Praise for
The Zen Priestess and the Snake

The Zen Priestess and the Snake is the journey of a deeply spiritual woman through the rigors of patriarchal Zen training, to the discovery and honoring of the sacred feminine. I trust her voice, she is genuine and this is an important book.

Lama Tsultrim Allione, author of
Women of Wisdom, Feeding Your Demons, and
Wisdom Rising: Journey into the Mandala of the Empowered Feminine

What happens when the sacred feminine erupts within a woman who is practicing in Zen's patriarchal lineages, expressed especially through its male-centered stories, leaders, and institutionalized forms that have long oppressed the feminine? In this compelling book, Roshi Shinko Perez recounts her irresistible spiritual journey as the sacred serpent of The Great Mother uncoils itself in the inimical terrain of the Zen patriarchy to find its full expression. With the keen eye of an archaeologist, Roshi Shinko recounts the trauma of personal and collective oppression of the feminine. Her spiritual journey gives rise to The Great Heart Way for integrating emotional energies and, in this book, she sets forth the Goddess Practices as a skillful means for bringing the sacred feminine home. This book is a must read for all those who long for the sacred feminine, for those who don't know that they are longing, and for those who seek full integration of The Great Mother within themselves for the benefit of all beings and the Earth.

Roshi Wendy Egyoku Nakao, Abbot Emeritus Zen Center of Los Angeles
and co-author of *The Book of Householder Koans*

Roshi Ilia Shinko Perez is Western Zen's Lady of Light, revealing the shadows we Zen practitioners still carry from old patriarchal traditions. Using her own life experience as teacher, she reminds us to honor the feminine, revive our connection with the Earth, celebrate rather than dismiss our intuitions and emotions, and choose the Path of Heart over the Path of the Samurai.

Roshi Eve Myonen Marko, co-author of *The Book of Householder Koans*

At a time of global upheaval and collective suffering, this book is a cup brimming with peaceful power. Roshi Shinko excavates and lifts up the hidden feminine wisdom jewels in her beloved Buddhist tradition, skillfully melding the dharma with ancient goddess teachings and setting it all in the matrix of her own richly told story of growing up in Puerto Rico as a girl on fire with the gifts and challenges of an awakened heart.

Mirabai Starr, author of
Caravan of No Despair: A Memoir of Loss & Transformation and
Wild Mercy: Living the Fierce & Tender Wisdom of the Women Mystics

This lively and valuable book, *The Zen Priestess and the Snake*, is essential reading for those who wish to enter the secret world of the divine feminine – where we are served a lush banquet of spiritual training from Mother Mary, The Zen Tea Ladies, Tibetan Dakinis, and the ancient Goddesses of Mesopotamia. We meet these amazing female spiritual teachers through their intimate relationships with the author, Zen Roshi Shinko Perez. Shinko encountered these spirit guides while galloping her mare along the ocean, painting in full color, and through practicing Zen and Tibetan Buddhism. We not only travel with her and the unearthed goddesses of archaeology and Buddhism, but we are offered practices to join these beings and heal ourselves in the vast sky of awakening.

Grace Schireson, author of
Zen Women: Beyond tea ladies, iron maidens and macho masters and *Naked in the Zendo*

For Zen to become the enlightening and healing tradition that we so urgently need today, it must outgrow its patriarchal roots and embrace the sacred feminine. Shinko Roshi is one of the pioneers showing us the way. A deep bow to her and this book, which blazes a new trail.

David Loy, author of *Ecodharma: Buddhist Teachings for the Ecological Crisis*

Shinko Roshi's intimate memoir movingly traces her recovery of the Sacred Feminine in her life through Zen practice, artistic expression, and shamanic teachings from old Tibet. Against the backdrop of her Puerto Rican roots, her Spanish childhood, and her adult American journey, she resolves to heal the damaging effects of patriarchy by teaching goddess practices for American Buddhism.

Judith Simmer-Brown, author of
Dakini's Warm Breath: The Feminine Principle in Tibetan Buddhism

The Zen Priestess and the Snake

I dedicate the merits of writing this book
To the well-being of our planet,
To the safety of all beings
And the natural world!

The Zen Priestess and the Snake

A Woman's Path of
Transformation and Healing
Through Rediscovery of
the Great Mother Tradition

Roshi Ilia Shinko Perez

THE ZEN PRIESTESS AND THE SNAKE
A Woman's Path of Transformation and Healing Through Rediscovery of the Great Mother Tradition
Roshi Ilia Shinko Perez

Text and illustrations © Roshi Ilia Shinko Perez 2020
Editing & design: John Negru
Cover painting: Ilia Shinko Perez
Author photo: Gerry Shishin Wick

ISBN: 978-1-896559-59-9

Published by
The Sumeru Press Inc.
Ottawa, ON
Canada

Library and Archives Canada Cataloguing in Publication

Title: The Zen priestess and the snake : a woman's path of transformation and healing through rediscovery of the great mother tradition / Roshi Ilia Shinko Perez.
Other titles: Woman's path of transformation and healing through rediscovery of the great mother tradition
Names: Perez, Ilia Shinko, author.
Description: Includes bibliographical references.
Identifiers: Canadiana 20200239694 | ISBN 9781896559599 (softcover)
Subjects: LCSH: Perez, Ilia Shinko—Religion. | LCSH: Meditation—Zen Buddhism. | LCSH: Meditation—
    Bon (Tibetan religion)
Classification: LCC BL627 .P37 2020 | DDC 294.3/4435—dc23

 For more information about The Sumeru Press
visit us at sumeru-books.com

Contents

Part I

Introduction

This book is about the recovery of the Sacred Feminine in the world and in myself. She arose from the realm of emptiness. This book, too, arose from the realm of emptiness and it is alive. Emptiness is the space where there is not a single thing. When I dissolve in emptiness, I become the one consciousness of all, bright and clear. The dissolution of my self in emptiness is the experience of nirvana, the cessation of suffering.

This is not a linear book. It is a spiral of endless time, of serpentine motion that comes from the beginning of beginning-less time. It is a Zen book. Not a patriarchal Zen book but a Zen book of the female priestess of all times.

My first spiritual initiation started with the experience of the Lady of Light when I was five-and-a-half years old. Many other "out of the ordinary" experiences followed this first one. Not only have I had blissful supernatural experiences, but I have also had difficult relationships in the personal and the spiritual fields that, with time, I was able to overcome. Thanks to my connection with the Lady of Light, the innocence of my two sons, and the energy of the horses that I have had throughout my life, I was able to never lose contact with my soul's life work. I do not use the word soul here to represent a static, eternal being in the sense used in the Abrahamic faiths, or the individuated karmic traveler of the Hindu faith. I use the word soul to mean the essence that emanates from the deepest chamber of my heart. It is used as a synonym of true self.

Work is very important in Zen. There is the story of Master Hyakujo. He was a great Zen master of the eighth and ninth centuries. At the monastery where he lived and taught Zen, he worked equally hard in the fields. The monks were alarmed to see him working hard under the scorching sun. They were concerned for his health since he was already 90 years old. In order to protect him, the monks hid his garden tools. He did not eat that day and hung up a sign on his door that read: "A day of no work is a day of no eating." The monks had to return his tools.

Work as mindfulness practice, the attention to details, has always been a great refuge for me. Absorption in work is a great way to forget the self and to be enlightened by the ten thousand things, as Zen Master Dogen proclaimed in the thirteenth century. The path of Zen is all about realizing what there is beyond the ego self. Zen saved my life.

For decades I was emotionally closed down in silence; Zen practice gave me the tools to undo my numbness and to discover who I was beyond the constricting walls of the conditioned self. The path of discovering who we are never ends. How much do you want to experience?

Walking through the streets of the Gothic City in Barcelona, where I have come to spend two months with my mother, I feel the sacred snake arising from the underground and raising her head to the open skies. She is rising through me. In prehistoric times the snake was a sacred symbol, the symbol of healing, clairvoyance and the Great Mother. In the centuries before the Christian era, the religion of the Great Mother was persecuted and it went underground. In the myth of Adam and Eve, the snake is degraded from a symbol of sacred healing to a symbol of evil and destruction. However, the snake as a healing symbol survived from ancient Greece in the emblem of the caduceus, which is still used by doctors and pharmacies to this day.

The snake represents our own power of clarity inside our body. Oh, but yes, the body was also turned into a source of sin during the Christian era, degraded from when it was a source of blissful communion with the creatrix of all life. However, the wisdom that is innate in our bodies cannot be destroyed. It is still here and together we can embark on the heroic task of saving the Earth.

Patriarchy turned everything upside down. Men and women living together in harmony was turned into the domination of women by men. Women's innate wisdom was seen as crazy or evil, something to fear and destroy. Women of wisdom who knew their own powers were burned as witches in medieval times. The care and communion with the Earth were turned into the exploitation of her resources and her creatures.

Now, when patriarchy is releasing its most ferocious attacks to continue destroying the Earth for the benefit of a few and at the expense of the many, like a dying dinosaur thrashing blindly with its large tail, it is time for the feminine wisdom in people of all genders to rise again.

The Earth is screaming for help louder than ever. Many of her creatures are extinct, the ice caps melting, the oceans rising, the Earth and the seas polluted, the ozone layer disappearing, fires of unprecedented proportions burning the forests, hurricanes of unheard magnitudes, frequent earthquakes and tsunamis, devastating floods, wars and starvation. Can you hear her cry yet?

In the *Tao Te Ching*, Lao Tzu writes,

> There was something formless and perfect
> before the universe was born.
> It is serene. Empty.
> Solitary. Unchanging.
> Infinite. Eternally present.
> It is the mother of the universe.
> For lack of a better name,
> I call it Tao. [Chapter 25]

Lao Tzu continues,

> When man interferes with Tao,
> the sky becomes filthy,
> the earth becomes depleted,
> the equilibrium crumbles,
> creatures become extinct. [Chapter 34]

It is time to wake up from the dream of ignorance, from the tale of lies we have been told that obscured the truth of who we really are, and from the lethargy of a life of fake comfort and security. It is time to speak the truth, to come together and to work for the vision of a renewed Earth, of new powers, in whatever way is available for each one of us. There is so much to do.

There is a joke about a man who died and went to a realm of leisure and indulgence. A butler tended to all of his needs. He only had to sit back in a recliner chair and relax all day long. He could order the most expensive meals, watch the best movies, drink the best wines and call for as many beautiful young maidens as he desired. One day, the man got bored of that afterlife and asked the butler, "Is there anything I can do in this place? If this is heaven, I would rather be in hell!" The butler exclaimed, "Where do you think you are, sir?"

Nirvana, the cessation of suffering, is something we can experience through the practice of *zazen* (sitting meditation). However, we cannot remain here. We always have to come back to this Earth and work for the benefit of all beings. This kind of work is true happiness, true joy and true freedom. As the Zen proverb says, "After enlightenment, the laundry." But it is more than the laundry. Enlightenment is working for all beings everywhere. After enlightenment, what can I do to help? Before enlightenment, what can I do to help?

The famous Zen Master Hakuin said, "This very land is the lotus land and this very body, the body of Buddha." This is a good vision to manifest together. Maha Prajna Paramita is the wisdom that takes us from the shore of suffering to the shore of enlightenment. Both shores are intrinsically the same but in order to see this, we need to realize it first. It is the bag of conditioning that the egotistic self carries that makes the pure lotus land into the land of suffering.

My life is a life of service. The survival of our planet and the survival of the human species are being threatened by the greed of corporations and oligarchs embarked on a crusade of extracting oil in the Arctic and Antarctic regions as the ice caps continue to melt. I offer my grief to our precious planet, our mother. I also ask her for forgiveness. Of all the abuse that we, people of all genders, have suffered, the Earth has been the most abused of all. Grief arises from love. We grieve when we lose what we love. Out of our grief, loving action arises. It takes courage to grieve. Grieving is selfless. When we do not grieve, we engage in the ego strategy of anger and hatred, and then depression and despair might set in. We become unable to act in accord with circumstances. Like the Buddha said: "Hatred does not cease through hatred at any time. Hatred ceases through love. This is an unalterable law."

One of the ways that loving action manifests in me is calling on the Lady of Light and visualizing her for inspiration, energy and inner vision. I use a method of *painting from the heart* to create visions of healing for the Earth, and I engage in the activist groups on climate emergency in my area including the Rocky Mountain Ecodharma movement, Extinction Rebellion Buddhists, Zen Teacher Climate Crisis Group, Zen Peacemaker Order and Longmont Vigil.

In the traditional Four Bodhisattva Vows, the *bodhisattva* vows to accomplish the impossible. In general terms, we can say that a bodhisattva is someone who vows to live and act with openness, courage and honesty for the well-being of others.

> Numberless creations, I vow to liberate,
> Inexhaustible delusions, I vow to dissolve,
> Omnipresent Dharma gates, I vow to experience,
> Unsurpassable enlightened way, I vow to manifest.

In his book *Ecodharma*, Zen Master David Loy creates a new term for the bodhisattva of today – the *ecosattva* – for bodhisattvas who are engaged in helping the Earth and bringing awareness to where we are heading if we do not change the direction we are going.

Jataka tales are stories written in India, between 300 BCE and 400 CE, regarding the previous lives of the Buddha in both human or animal form. There is a story about a little bird that I have adapted from the Jataka tales, which illustrates the spirit of the ecosattva. The forest is on fire. All the animals are running for their lives. Many of them will die and many trees will be lost. There is a little bird who, upon seeing this, embarks on the impossible task of putting out the fire and saving all animals in the forest. In her little beak she brings drops of water from a nearby creek and drops them on the fire. Other animals see her and laugh at her and try to discourage her. The little bird with her scorched feathers continues bringing drops of water to put out the fire, at the risk of her own life. Enlightened beings of the universe, seeing this, gather clouds of rain above the fire. Rain pouring from the sky puts the fire out.

This is a nice story that, in a metaphorical way, illustrates the power of the heart and the vow of the bodhisattva or ecosattva to save all sentient beings and the Earth. This is my vow as well.

I hope that you can sense the heartbeat of Mother Earth, the galloping of the horse and the uncoiling of the snake through the pages of this book.

Maha Prajna Paramita!

1

Paradise

I am 11 years old and in a classroom; I don't remember exactly what kind of subject they are teaching, something that doesn't interest me. Everything they teach is out of touch with my life and my inner reality. I look out of the window into the blue sky and into the white puffy clouds passing by in the luminous immensity. I see life there; I see energy there.

Here in this classroom all seems lifeless. The nuns try to kill all spontaneity and any manifestation of innocence. Even joy seems to be taboo. I look again out of the window with nostalgia for those days when I was truly alive: those days when there was no separation between the world and me.

I see a pinkish radiance all around me. I feel loved and safe. I am delighted and intrigued by it at the same time. Even the clouds are tinted with this soft red light. I understand now that this light was the energy of love that was wrapped around me. I hear a voice inside me speaking. It is not a voice that is separate from my body. It is a voice that comes from my body and speaks in a way as if the sky had opened up inside me and is manifesting itself in words: "You will understand later, when you are old."

In my child's mind I interpret being old being, like, 40 years old! But when I reached 40, I still didn't understand. Only a few fragments were clear. The rest was obscured in great doubt. I had a great doubt because my full experience had not yet been realized. I felt like I was following an ethereal path. Often, the active conceptual mind of the ego-self tried to convince me that the path was foolish, or useless or unproductive. And yet, in spite of all these doubts, I always trusted my heart's intuitive non-conceptual wisdom. Thanks to my Zen training, I developed great faith in that which cannot be comprehended intellectually, and this faith allowed me not to lose my way and to continue with my inner search.

At age 50 the mass of doubt had become lighter. As I write this today, I am 65 years old and finally I do understand that which is beyond understanding. Sometime in my life, past, present and future intersected, becoming one timeless experience. When I was a little girl, I had a vivid experience of the unconditional love of the Divine Feminine as a manifestation of the Lady of Light. At 65, I teach these ancient Goddess Practices. When I do these practices,

I visualize myself as the Lady of Light. Was it me as the Lady of Light in the future who saved me when I was a little girl? And when I was growing up, was it my future self as the Lady of Light who guided me on the path to becoming Her in the future?

I came from a childhood paradise of free and lively energy. It was also alive with sexual energy. Until I was five-and-a-half years old, I lived a very happy life with my parents in a house in the tropical forest of Puerto Rico. We had several acres of land, all cultivated with tropical fruits. When I was four years old, my parents gave me my first horse; his name was Cariño, a very sweet and tamed gelding that I used to ride fearlessly at that young age. In this land there were also lots of animals that roamed freely; they were happy animals, not exploited. Everything was full of life. The thought of death had not entered my mind yet, or sin or even wrongdoing. My parents were not into religion and they had not instructed me with any religious doctrine. All I knew was that life was expansive and everything was alive in its own goodness. In the tropical forest of Puerto Rico there were no dangerous animals. The days were always splendid. Everything was as you would imagine the Garden of Eden was.

There was a dark-skinned boy who lived next to our property in a slum, or *caserío*, as it was called in Puerto Rico. Our property was separated from the caserío by a wire fence. The boy, Héctor, and I used to stand on each side of the fence and press our bodies together. I still remember with great intensity the amount of electricity that was unleashed by my body, transporting me into a realm of pure bliss. This blissful electricity was the supreme nectar of my paradise.

Sometimes Héctor would squeeze through the wire fence and come to play. We had made a tent of discarded fabric and sticks. Sometimes, when we were alone and no one was watching, he would lie down on top of me. Suddenly, I would enter again into the realm of pure bliss. We would remain immobile, feeling the intensity of this ecstasy. We didn't touch with our hands or kiss. There was no guilt in my mind yet or even the idea of misconduct. Everything was alive in this Puerto Rican paradise – the luscious trees with all different kinds of tropical fruits, the free roaming animals and the aliveness of innocent sexuality.

2

End of Paradise and the Lady of Light

When I was five-and-a-half years old, my paradise collapsed. It happened when I had to start kindergarten. Since we lived in the country and there were no schools nearby, my parents needed to relocate to the city of San Juan. While they were relocating, they decided to let me live at my grandparents' house. They had a beautiful house in San Juan in a neighborhood of colonial houses called Miramar. My grandmother had a sister. We called her Titi. My grandmother's parents adopted Titi when she was a little girl. Although Titi was part of the family, she worked for the family as a kind of governess. She had helped raise my mother and now she was helping to raise me. For the most part, she was a wonderful woman, a second grandmother to me.

Titi had a big bedroom on the backside of the house which opened to an inner garden. I was assigned to sleep in the same room with her. In Titi's room there were two twin beds that formed an L-shape with a table in between. I slept in one of those beds and Titi in the other. The bedroom was big and had three doors. One door opened to a good-sized bathroom tiled in different tones of blue; another had a huge key always inside the lock of the door that connected Titi's room to my grandparents' house; and the third door opened to a courtyard garden. This was my favorite door. The garden was beautiful, with tropical plants that had heart-shaped leaves as big as me and trumpet vines with flowers of a pale yellow tone that stood out in the bright blue sky. These flowers were magical to me and inspired in me the feeling of growing up inside a fairy tale.

I started kindergarten at a well-known Catholic school in Miramar called El Perpetuo Socorro, run by nuns. I felt lost there. I missed my country paradise and my home with my parents.

In the neighbor's house, there lived a boy my own age who went to kindergarten with me. His name was Gilberto. We became friends and we used to play together after school. One day, while we were playing together in the backyard of his house, he said he had to pee. He pulled down his zipper and started to pee just to my side. He didn't bother to cover himself. He was peeing so close to me that I could clearly see his little penis. I had never seen that before. Coming from my house in the tropical forest with all of the animals that I used to play with, I thought that he had taken a very small animal out of his zipper. In my innocent mind, I asked, "Can I touch it?" He said, "Yes." I quickly touched it with the tip of my index finger. I wasn't sure if the little creature would bite me or not. Then we continued playing.

It just so happened that Gilberto's older brother saw this incident and went to tell Titi. I have no idea what he told her and much less what she understood. Titi was a devout Catholic and had been a spinster all of her life. She was short in stature with light dark skin and the soft and yet angular fixtures of the Taíno Indian. The Taíno Indians were the indigenous people who populated Puerto Rico before the arrival of the Spanish Conquistadors. I was told in school that the Taínos were a peaceful tribe. They were enslaved by the conquistadors and made to perform very hard tasks in the gold mines of the island. Because they were not used to hard labor, many of them died and others were killed. No pure Taíno blood survived and what remained was mixed with the blood of the conquistadors. However, Titi must have had a large percentage of Taíno blood. Unfortunately, my recent DNA test showed I have only five percent.

Titi dressed in conservative clothing, usually wearing nylon skirts and dresses that reached to below her knees. Although Titi was sweet and caring most of the time, she could be self-righteous and judgmental.

On that unfortunate afternoon with Gilberto, Titi came to get me and, taking me by the arm, pushed me into her room.

"You have committed a mortal sin," she yelled at me. "Now you are going to hell. The hellish flames will devour you." She added that I was a disgrace to the family and that my mother had never done anything like that. My mind was innocent and I did not know exactly what was wrong. Therefore, I could not defend myself. My mind totally fixated on the flames of hell that were going to consume me alive.

There was a church next to the school, and Titi made me go to Mass on Sundays with her ever since I had arrived. I didn't understand anything regarding the Mass or why we had to go there, but I paid attention to the terrifying frescos on the church walls. These frescos were very realistic and of huge proportions, at least in the eyes of a young girl. They depicted the souls in purgatory in terrible suffering, being devoured by flames that reached above their waists. Those souls were in great torment. This imagery had nothing to do with how I had experienced paradise in my home in the country. I was shocked by these images.

Titi probably had explained the meaning of the frescos to me at some point, because I did know the difference between purgatory and hell. As far as I know, she had never seen a penis in her life and projected onto me, an innocent girl of five-and-a-half, all of the sexual repression she had accumulated through the years. She must have been somewhere in her fifties at that time. The very moment she said to me I was going to burn in hell, I wholeheartedly believed it.

In my vivid imagination, I saw terrifying waves of fire wrapping all over me. I felt acute terror and my whole body shook with fear while I envisioned the flames of hell all around me. I couldn't stop crying and yelling in terror. I entered hell totally.

If I thought that purgatory was bad, I imagined hell would be much worse. The flames would be a lot bigger and there wouldn't be the possibility for redemption. With my mind's eye, I saw myself being devoured thoroughly by the flames of hell. I was alone without any defense or protection. I didn't question Titi or blame her or defend myself in any way. I was told I was going to burn in hell, and I did. My mind's visions were so real that I felt acute terror. I screamed in tears while sitting on my bed. I don't know how long this lasted, but no one came to console me at all.

It wasn't dark when my aunt condemned me so she must have left the bedroom and came back when I was already asleep, exhausted from the panic, the yelling and the crying of seeing myself burning in hell.

I don't know how I woke up, but the next thing I remember is sitting up peacefully on my bed next to Titi's bed, where she lay asleep. From my bed, I saw in the center of the room, between our beds, the image of the most magnificent woman you can imagine. She was made of light, floating above the ground in some sort of white energy that resembled white clouds, and the clouds were moving too. Nothing was static. Her attire was made of different shades of transparent light blue and white veils that moved as if there were wind in the room. Her face and hands were light golden. The most incredible thing was that this woman emanated from her entire body an incredible amount of love for me. I was bathed in love. In and out and through me there was only love, clarity and incredible beauty. I was wrapped completely in it. I don't know how long we stayed like this; these things are outside of time.

I stayed contemplating Her until I had the idea of sharing this beauty with Titi and touched her gently to wake her up. The lady made a gesture of silence, by bringing one finger up to her mouth in a silent "Shh!" But already Titi was awake. All I could say to Titi was, "Look Titi, Santa Claus!" It was too late; the lady had disappeared. Titi did not get to see the Lady of Light. She seemed very frightened as if I had seen a ghost. She tucked me in bed with her and covered both of us inside her sheets and blankets. I could feel Titi's fear while she wrapped herself around my body. I felt uncomfortable when she did that, but I didn't reject her because she seemed terribly frightened and wrapping herself around my body must have given her comfort. I felt tremendously loved by the Lady of Light and I fell asleep with a softness in my heart.

I remember how happy I was in the morning, running up and down in my grandparents' house and yelling, "I've seen Santa Claus! I've seen Santa Claus!"

Titi must have called my mother and asked her to come. My parents were still living in the house in the country, trying to relocate to San Juan and I didn't see them very often. It was certainly unusual to see my parents early in the morning in my grandparents' house. Even though they had to drive to see us early in the morning, my mother looked beautiful and elegant like a model, just as she always did. She must have been a bit concerned that morning, but I don't remember her being upset with me. Nor was she affectionate. What I do remember clearly is that no one appreciated my sighting of "Santa Claus," especially when my description didn't match their idea of Santa Claus but sounded more like the Virgin Mary. They made it clear to me that I should not talk about it again.

As a girl of five-and-a-half, I didn't understand what was wrong with the adults that they couldn't see or didn't want to see the amount of love and joy I was feeling and how extraordinary what had happened to me was. I couldn't fathom why they couldn't accept the beautiful Lady of Light.

The adults didn't say anything to me about whom they thought I had seen, but when my father started singing me a song about the Virgin Mary, I realized they had identified what I saw as the Virgin. I am sure that my father's intention was to be playful with me, but I took his singing as mockery. I felt very vulnerable and ashamed when my father sang to me, "Y la Virgen va de paso con su esposo hacia Belén" or "And the Virgin is passing by with her husband on their way to Bethlehem."

It seemed to me that he obviously had no idea what I had endured all by myself and he'd made it into something to joke about. This only increased my feeling of being a total stranger in the world of the adults. I never doubted that what I saw was the true reality and I felt sorry that the adults couldn't see it. I forgave them.

At that time, however, a message came to me from the same universal dimension that I intuitively knew the beautiful lady came from: "It is okay for you to forget about what you saw for the time being. You will understand later when you are old." I heard and saw this message in my mind's eye. There was a knowing beyond any doubt that came with it. I saw the spatial quality of the words in the absence of noise and movement. I knew this was the voice of beings of light, although I had never heard them before. When they spoke, everything became very still and I saw their words imbued with light.

Much later, when I was in my late fifties, I was drawn to read the *Avatamsaka Sutra*, and there I found and studied the bodhisattva stages. In the latest stages, the bodhisattvas are guided by the ascended mahasattvas. Mahasattvas, or enlightening beings, are beings made of light who enlighten others with their presence and their voice. This was my experience. Although there was only one voice, I knew there were many "enlightening" beings included in the one voice. *Enlightening* is the term used in the *Avatamsaka Sutra* to name all the enlightened beings of the universe. I like this term enlightening very much because it doesn't attribute a self to the experience of enlightenment.

I never forgot about the Lady of Light, but I did forget about Titi's abuse and all of the suffering that I went through. Eventually the abuse became unconscious and I didn't remember it at all. Later on, I wrote in *The Great Heart Way* – the book I co-authored with Gerry Shishin Wick Roshi – that as children, when we go through some traumatic event, the wisdom of our

24

body can kick in and put that memory out of conscious reach so that we can continue functioning normally. Also, thanks to the practice explained in our book, I was able to heal that hidden trauma. I did continue to love Titi, but I didn't feel close or affectionate towards her. It was much later, when I was in my mid-forties, that I understood that Titi had actually been a bodhisattva in my life. Thanks to her, I was able to enter the dimension of light.

There is a beautiful poem in the *Blue Cliff Record*, case 18, that says,

> South of Sho and North of Tan,
> Yellow gold within fills the whole country.
> A ferry boat under the shadowless tree,
> Up in the crystal palace, there is no one who knows.
> [Cleary, *Secrets of the Blue Cliff Record*, Case 18]

"South of Sho and North of Tan" means everywhere. "Yellow gold within fills the whole country" means that our true nature is so rich that it fills the whole universe.

In "A ferry boat under the shadowless tree," the ferryboat refers to the Mahayana or the path of the bodhisattva that carries people from the shore of delusion to the shore of enlightenment. Enlightenment is the shadowless tree, the tree under which the Buddha was enlightened. In other words, this whole line means that enlightenment is available to everyone.

"Up in the crystal palace, there is no one who knows" refers to the *Sambhogakaya* realm, the realm of light or Buddha fields. The bodhisattva can enter this realm with her ability to transcend the ordinary knowing of the ego mind – "there is no one who knows."

The crystal palace is full of light, reflecting light, absorbing light. A crystal palace is a perfect metaphor for the Sambhogakaya. The *Blue Cliff Record* is the second book of koans that we study in the Zen lineage of Harada-Yasutani, which is both *Rinzai* and *Soto*. The lineage of Harada-Yasutani includes the attention to detail and mindfulness practice of the Soto lineage and the vigorous practice of koans of the Rinzai tradition. Koans are the non-dual sayings of the great Zen masters of old times, and I'll talk more about koans later.

When I was nine years old, my parents separated, and my mother, siblings and I moved to Spain. Titi came with us to look after my younger sisters. My father stayed in Puerto Rico.

In Madrid, I went to another Catholic school run by nuns. The nuns made everyone go to church. In the church there was a beautiful sculpture of the Virgin Mary. Sculpted in white marble, she was about five feet tall or so. She was dressed in white and light blue robes. I used to contemplate her beauty because she – like the images of *Guan Yin*, the Chinese Goddess of Mercy, I would encounter later in life – reminded me of the beautiful and loving lady who came to my rescue on the terrible day when I'd felt myself burning in hell. However, there was something about this statue that didn't match the energy of the Lady of Light. This Virgin Mary statue with a tender and loving face was crushing the head of a black snake beneath her feet. I didn't understand until much later the reason for this aggression toward the snake and I was afraid to ask at the time.

Although my father stayed in Puerto Rico, I used to visit him in the summers. Years before my parents' separation, my grandfather had bought a house for my family on the shore of a private beach an hour north of San Juan. This place was even more magical than anywhere I had seen before. My grandfather was a prominent and compassionate doctor. He had made some good investments when he bought the beach house; later on he lost everything and our family felt the loss of financial security, but that is a different part of my story.

One day, while I was playing with my younger siblings in front of the beach house, a young man passed by riding on a nice-looking horse. My father asked the man, Geño, "Is the mare for sale?" Geño assented. My father bought the mare for me and I named her Niña. That was the best present of my entire life. I used to take her into the ocean with me and we would swim together. I would ride with or without a saddle and with just a rope on her neck. Next to our beach there was another beach. It was isolated and wild. I could gallop with my mare at high speed on that beach and I would stand up with both feet on one of the stirrups and then repeat on the other side. Or I would just stand with both feet on the saddle as we galloped. As we galloped, the huge fans of palm trees filtered the sunlight that caressed my face as the multicolor crabs disappeared into the bushes. Thousands of purple, orange and red crabs scurried to hide at a synchronized and harmonious pace. The multitude of sounds from waves, plants, birds, insects and frogs created a symphonic melody such as I have never heard again.

There are no words to describe the amount of freedom I felt riding my mare. We were one. Her movements were my movements and my movements were her movements. There was no danger. This was a very important time in my life. My mare connected me with the Lady of Light. I knew who I was when I was with her. I didn't have a name. I was essence. I was my own essence. Later in life I would learn it was my dakini essence. In her book *Women of Wisdom*, Tsultrim Allione describes the dakini essence:

> I realize now that, for me, spirituality is connected to a delicate, playful, spacious part of myself, which closes up in militant regimented situations. The more I try to limit my mind in outward forms, the more this subtle energy escapes like a shy young girl. It is as if I need to trust the vastness of my mind and let go, let my shoulders drop, not try to control situations, and yet not follow rampant discursive thoughts or hold on when my mind gets fixated. I think that this luminous, subtle spiritual energy is what is meant by the dakini principle. She is the key, the gate opener, and the guardian of the unconditioned primordial state, which is innate in everyone. If I am not willing to play with her, or if I try to force her, or if I do not invoke her, the gate remains closed and I remain in darkness and ignorance.

When I was studying in middle school in Spain, my family took a trip to France and visited the Grotto of the Virgin of Lourdes. There I was with my mother and my aunt and my younger siblings. I vividly remember thinking, "I can't believe it! Here they are, my mother and my aunt, admiring the place where a girl of 14 saw the Young Lady, as the shepherdess girl called her." And there they were, admiring the apparition that happened to the shepherdess girl, named Bernadette.

I was so disturbed; I couldn't say anything. I wanted to yell, "BUT WHAT ABOUT ME? What about the beautiful Lady of Light who appeared to me in your own house? What about that?"

But no, I said nothing. I felt insignificant and without a voice. Then I learned that Bernadette had chosen to live a secluded, almost cloistered life. I do too for the most part live a secluded, almost cloistered life. The following description of her "Young Lady" matched perfectly how I felt and how I still feel about my Lady of Light,

> So lovely, when you have seen her once,
> You would willingly die to see her again.
> [Taylor, *Bernadette of Lourdes: Her Life, Death and Visions*]

However, Bernadette said that her Young Lady told her that She was the immaculate conception. She also said that she carried a rosary and yellow flowers on her feet and asked Bernadette to pray for the sinners. My Lady of Light did not condemn sexuality, she did not say anything about being immaculate, nor was she wearing a rosary, nor did she ask me to pray for the sinners. She only emanated great love.

In his translation of the *Tao Te Ching*, Stephen Mitchell writes:

> The teaching of the *Tao Te Ching* is moral in its deepest sense. Unencumbered by any concept of sin, the Master doesn't see evil as a force to resist, but simply as an opaqueness, a state of self-absorption which is in disharmony with the universal process, so that, as with a dirty window, the light can't shine through.

When I was 12 years old, my mare Niña passed away. My mare, in a way, carried my soul. I could be who I truly was when I galloped with her. I could enjoy the sense of heightened clarity without a self and be wild, courageous and free. When she died, that part of me remained suspended in time like in a standby mode.

When I was 13 years old, my father passed away. My father was everything to me. He was my biggest support and encouragement in life. When my parents were separating, I had gone with my brother and my mother to live in Madrid. Puerto Rico was a beautiful and prosperous island 55 years ago, a real jewel. It was hard for me to live in Spain in that time of the dictator Francisco Franco, but it was magical to go back to the island during my school vacations and be with my father and my mare. Now that he died, I felt as if I had no one.

I connected intimately with my mother when we first moved to Spain. We moved to Spain in two different waves while my parents were separating. First, my brother and I moved there with my mother. Titi remained in Puerto Rico with my younger sisters and my father. My mother was in her early thirties when she came to Spain to study in two majors; one was philosophy and the other was fine arts. She already had a degree in science, but she had discovered that it was not her path. My grandfather encouraged her to pursue her true interest and he supported all of us while we were in Spain. My mother had found a house with a garden for us in Madrid at a time in Spain when having a backyard was very rare. This was when I got to know intimately my mother's sweet and tender heart, and that connection lasts to these days.

She always protected me when the nuns complained about my behavior, and I think she secretly liked my independence and curious mind. My classmates loved my mother because she dressed in modern fashions, looking as elegant as royalty and slightly aloof. In return, I enjoyed her fellow students when she brought them to the house to do art projects. I often joined in the art with those young, fun people. Even though she was always so busy with her studies, she took good care of me. She always supervised the help who cleaned the house and cooked the meals for us.

I wasn't able to continue enjoying that kind of intimacy with her when Titi came to join us with the rest of my siblings. I did love all of my siblings, but they were younger than me and I couldn't share intimately with them. I felt alone all through puberty.

When my father died in a motorboat accident in San Juan, I became numb. I did not feel his death because something in me just shut down. I became like my own ghost. When my father's death happened and it was announced in my school, the other girls pointed at me. I felt I was different and that I didn't belong anymore. I had lost my friends, my mare and my father.

I took refuge in painting and in sports. I was the captain of the school team of *balonmano*, or handball, which is like a hybrid between basketball and soccer. I put the team together. There was another school next to ours. It was a school for poor girls that the nuns sponsored. I found these girls a lot nicer than the rich girls who were my classmates. I became friends with them and we formed the team together. We won a championship and a trophy. No one ever came to see me play or came to any of the games during the championship except for my brother Tito. I loved my brother very much then and now.

Every evening when I came back from school, I painted with my watercolors, markers and crayons. It was during one of my painting sessions that I received another message from the enlightening beings: "You will be doing this kind of painting when you grow up." Painting kept me sane. As part of the Great Heart Way, we have been incorporating process painting. In process painting, the experience of painting is more important than the outcome. The goal is the creative act itself without concerns for talent, skills or the final product. Process painting can allow you to go beyond the limitations of conceptual thinking and enter into an inner journey of intuition, feelings and transformation. It was also thanks to the Great Heart Way that I was able to undo my numbness and grieve the death of my father and my mare.

3

Who Am I?

Subsequently I grew up, graduated as an archaeologist from the University Autónoma of Madrid, married, moved to the United States, had a full-time job and had two children. I had not practiced any religion since I was 14 years old and I did not believe in a God. Once in a while I did pray to the Lady of Light.

When I was 30 years old, I started my formal Zen practice. Zen is a spiritual discipline based on sitting meditation, or zazen. A friend introduced me to this discipline by giving me a book called *The Three Pillars of Zen* by Roshi Philip Kapleau. In this book, I read that the mind can be trained through the practice of meditation and we can reconnect again with our internal silence. This touched me deeply. I had noticed how over the years, my mind had become busier and busier. I felt as if I carried a cassette player in my head all the time and I couldn't stop it, day or night. I was hungry for silence and Zen practice provided me with the door to reconnect with my original silence. Silence became more than just silence – I could feel stillness, spaciousness and clarity within the silence.

Another thing that Zen practice gave me that fit me so well was the koan "Who am I?" As I mentioned briefly before, koans are the sayings of the great Zen masters of old times which have been recorded in several books and are used to expand the minds of Zen students. Each koan presents a paradox that must be solved by the awakening of the non-dualistic dimension of who we are.

For example, in the koan called "Joshu sees through the two hermits," Zen Master Joshu, a famous Chinese Zen master from the ninth century, approaches a hermit's hut and asks the hermit, "Are you in? Are you in?" The hermit responds by lifting up his fist. Joshu replies, "The water is too shallow here to anchor a vessel." And he walks away. Then Joshu goes to the second hermit's hut and asks again, "Are you in? Are you in?" This hermit also lifts up his fist. Joshu replies, "You are free to give or to take away." And Joshu bows to this hermit. [Shibayama, *Zen Comments on the Mumonkan*, Case 11] This koan is about equanimity.

Zen koans cannot be revealed with conceptual explanations. In solving a koan, we are encouraged to forget about our ego self and to feel that we are the hermits and Joshu. You, as the first hermit, how do you respond when Joshu asks you if you are in? Then you, as Joshu, what do you say to the first hermit after he lifted his fist? You have to express your understanding of the words and actions of Joshu and the hermit in order to reveal the teaching of equanimity that is happening here. Then you repeat the same process with the second hermit and Joshu.

There is a verse about equanimity in the *Tao Te Ching* that says,

> When people see some things as beautiful,
> Other things become ugly.
> When people see some things as good,
> Other things become bad. [Chapter 2]

If you do not see a koan at first glance, when you go to see your Zen teacher in the private interview known as *dokusan*, she or he might give you some direction on how to work with it. However, the practice of koans does not start with koans like "Joshu sees through the two hermits." The practice starts with koans called "breakthrough koans." The most common breakthrough koans are, "What is your original face before your parents were born?" "What is Mu?" "Who am I?" or "What is the sound of one hand?"

The koan "Who am I?" given to me by my first teacher Philip Kapleau and his successor Bodhin Kjolhede was very healing for me. It was the gateway through which I returned to my true lost home. Inspired by Kapleau's book, *The Three Pillars of Zen*, I signed up for all the retreats that were offered at the Rochester Zen Center in New York, founded by Kapleau. The way that I was taught to work with "Who am I?" was to use it in every exhalation. Before using a koan, the concentration in our breathing must be strong. We must be able to inhale and exhale from our *hara*, an area of the lower abdomen, without losing focus on the breathing.

First, I inhaled deeply from the hara, then while I exhaled a very deep and long breath, I added the sound whoooooooooooooooo? to it. The duration of this sound should be as long as the duration of the exhalation. I tell my students that the sound of whoooooooooooooo? should be no louder than the whisper of a secret to oneself.

This koan or any other koans are not to be used to develop complicated conceptual answers. In order to answer a koan, we must let go of the control of wanting to know what to say and enter into the uncharted territory of the *not knowing* mind. It is crucial to have a teacher when you are working with a koan.

It was during a retreat, while I was working with the koan "Who am I?" that I felt a lot of fear moving through me. I had no one to share this with. In the lineage of Philip Kapleau, we were not allowed to bring personal issues to the teacher during dokusan. You either knew the answer to your koan or you were dismissed from the room immediately.

Each retreat I attended at the Rochester Zen Center had about sixty participants. We had dokusan three times a day in intervals of two hours. The time in the dokusan room was brief, usually lasting a few seconds, but not everyone would go to dokusan each time. The dokusan room was small, but decorated elegantly in a traditional Zen Japanese style. Wooden dividers, scrolls, bamboo wallpaper, wooden floors and soft light created the atmosphere for the exotic and mysterious encounters that took place there.

While we were sitting in meditation and when the teacher was ready to start the interview process, he would ring his dokusan bell. Immediately, a stampede of people wanting to see him would run up the stairs as fast as they could to find a place on a long line of cushions that were perfectly lined up in a large open room on the second floor.

I was very competitive then. Waiting for the bell to ring, I felt myself transforming energetically into a feline ready to jump at the first sound. I was sitting on an elevated platform in the middle aisle. I always arranged my cushion and my robes in a way that didn't interfere with my legs and could facilitate my jump. Not knowing what was going to happen once the bell rang made it razor-edge exciting for me. The sound of the bell! I had jumped as far as I could and advanced in front of several men. This thrill connected me with my soul's free galloping mare and the jungle. I could connect again with the feeling of riding my mare in the wild beach by the forest and also with the sense of heightened clarity without a self. I have traced this thread of connecting with my "soul's free galloping mare" through my entire life. And it was this thread of connection with the horse that allowed me not to completely lose contact with my true self in difficult times. I could always return here.

The person who got to the second floor first was to enter directly into the dokusan room. The rest of the people would sit on the line of cushions starting at the front of the line where there was a large bell. When the teacher rang his bell, the person in front of the line had to hit the bell three times. There should be no gap between the teacher's bell ringing and the student's bell answering. A good teacher can tell the state of mind of the student by the sound of the bell. The best way to come to dokusan is being empty. It took me a while to learn to become empty. Being empty, the boundaries between me, the bell and the present moment started to dissolve and then there was just awareness itself.

When you sit in front of the teacher you are really sitting very close to them. No wonder it is called "face to face" – you are really in front of the face of the teacher and they are right in front of your face. After stating my name and my practice, the teacher waited for a few seconds. Perceiving that I hadn't had a breakthrough experience, or *kensho*, yet, he would reach for the hand bell on the floor next to his zabuton and ring it. Once the bell rang, I knew I had to exit.

When I was releasing the unconscious memory of Titi's abuse, I felt intense fear that lasted for days. C.G. Jung wrote, "Meditation…seems to be the royal road to the unconscious mind." But I did not know then that meditation is the royal road to the unconscious mind. However, I was soon going to find out. Working whole-heartedly with my koan "Who am I?" I was aware that I had started a journey into the depth of my mind. The koan was everything to me. I wanted to know with all my might who I was beyond appearances, credentials, age and gender. Who was I as essence? This questioning was more important than my own life. During one retreat at the Rochester Zen Center, I went through what I now call a mental storm. I had all kinds of thoughts; some were even half thoughts, an interminable quantity of discombobulated thoughts. I even had voices of people in my head and I did not know who they were. I felt my head had become like one of those black-and-white TVs from the 1960s…when the reception was bad, all you saw on the screen were scrambled images and you heard strange voices among the white noise as you changed the channels trying to find one that worked. The next time I went to see the teacher in dokusan, I told him I thought I was going crazy. In a jovial and friendly manner Bodhin Sensei told me, "No, you are not going crazy. The mind is like a toilet; when you flush it, a lot of shit gets stirred up until it goes away."

This was very helpful and reassuring to me. I continued putting all of my attention in the koan and my breath. The next day, I felt that all of my out-of-control thoughts, noises and voices were gone. I felt very light in my body almost as if I could fly. I felt very happy from within. I had connected with myself at a deeper level and I felt that I had started the journey to return to my true lost home.

Until that time I had endured endless sessions of meditation in which I was placed in one of the "hot seats" in the *zendo*, or meditation room. The hot seats were on both sides of the central aisle and were reserved for those who were expected to have a breakthrough soon. Before the teacher rang his bell upstairs, announcing the start of dokusan, one of the monitors would give a short speech, usually about death. Then the two monitors would grab their *kyosakus*, narrow Zen paddles, from the altar. After bowing to the altar, to each other and to the participants, they would enter into a kind of frenzy —yelling "mu" while hitting avidly everyone sitting in the middle aisle. The hitting was not a punishment. It was about hitting some acupressure points in the shoulders to release tension and to keep students alert. This technique originated in Japan.

I had so much fire energy in me that I didn't need to be hit with the kyosaku. My shoulders got very sore from the hitting. Luckily my job during work period, *samu*, was to fold laundry. I used to take some wash towels, fold them and use them to cover my shoulders under my robe during meditation. It was only after I had my first breakthrough, or kensho experience, that I felt the freedom to tell one of the teachers that I did not want to be hit again.

The fact that they didn't allow the participants to talk about emotional difficulties during the retreat had a deep effect on me. I saw two women coming into the retreat looking sane and then I saw them coming out of the retreat looking insane; they had to undergo psychiatric treatment. I also saw many men stuck in their practice for many years. I am convinced that the reason for this was that their emotional bodies were not being addressed by the teachers. I even heard of a man who committed suicide in the middle of a retreat in Rochester. I myself had to go through a lot of terror without having anyone to guide me through it.

It was in the next retreat, when my mind had gotten very calm, that I felt a lot of fear being released from my body. I had no idea what this fear was about. Since there were no thoughts in my mind and I knew I could not bring emotional issues to the teacher, I concentrated on my koan, which I had intuitively adapted to "Who is feeling this?" This koan was my only companion through the many hours of zazen and I embraced it completely. Always inquiring, "Who is feeling this?" and at the same time feeling the old sensations of fear. I had no stories or thoughts in my mind, only the experience of fear in my body and the koan in my mind and heart. Fear turned into terror. I remember shaking with terror and at the same time not letting the koan go, while the cold shivering waves of terror moved through my entire body.

Then the live memory of the hellish flames came back. I once more experienced the memory of the little girl alone with mortal terror and also the vivid memory of the loving lady that came to my rescue. I came to realize it was due to my ability to trust my feelings without making stories about them that I was able as a child to connect with the Lady of Light.

After an intense day and night of feeling the old terror, everything returned to calm. I had gone through a dark night of the soul and in the morning I knew who I was. I presented the answer to the koan to the teacher. Taking his teaching stick as if it were a measuring tape, he said, "Full enlightenment is this whole stick, you are about here." He indicated the top part of the stick with his hands, and then placed one hand three-quarters up the stick. That measurement never made any sense to me, but it did not matter either. I was feeling so happy and grateful. A lot of burden had fallen from my mind. I had a vision at the time it happened. I saw a mountain of words and ideas crumbling down. Then I experienced freedom to act and speak. Until then I had felt captive of my own mind.

The teacher assigned me to work with miscellaneous koans. Miscellaneous koans are a number of koans used to teach people how to work with them before entering in the first book of koans called the *Mumonkan* or *Gateless Gate*.

The miscellaneous koans were very liberating for me. I vividly remember the first one of them, "How to stop the sound of the distant temple bell?" It was such a big pleasure to forget about the self and just become a bell completely and be just the sound that reverberates through the mountain hills endlessly. The self is so constricting with its identity and its conditioning, its role in society and so on. The koans allowed me to expand and experience the empty space, the background that is always open and available, in which the drama of the self occurs.

There is a legend about the emptiness of a Zen Master named Tozan. The gods wanted to see him, but they couldn't because he was empty. They would enter into him and pass through him, but they could not see him. They were very curious to see a man who had become empty, so they played a trick on him. When Tozan had gone for a walk, they went to the kitchen of the monastery where he lived. Taking a few handfuls of rice and wheat, they threw them on his path. In a Zen monastery, that action is very disrespectful to the rice and wheat. Everything should be respected because everything is alive. In a Zen monastery nothing is wasted; one should be careful and alert. When Tozan returned, he could not believe that any of his disciples could have been so careless and disrespectful. This idea arose in him because he felt offended, and suddenly a self was there and the gods could see him. He wasn't empty anymore. Suddenly an idea had crystallized. For a moment a cloud appeared in the blue sky and the gods could see him. Then the cloud disappeared because the idea disappeared. The gods again couldn't see him.

4

The Great Mother Gives Birth to Zen

When I encountered the writing of Torei Zenji, a Japanese Zen master from the eighteenth century, I felt I had found someone who really understood how I felt about many things. In his poem "The Bodhisattva Vow," he uses the word "Tathagata" to name the Buddha:

> When we regard the nature of all living creatures and all things, we find them to be the sacred forms of the Tathagata's never-failing essence. Each particle of matter, each moment, is no other than the Tathagata's inexpressible radiance. With this realization, our noble ancestors, possessed of compassionate minds and hearts, gave tender care to birds and beasts. And in our own daily lives we, too, should be reverently grateful for the protections of life: our food, drink and clothing! Though these are inanimate things, they are nonetheless the warm flesh and blood, the merciful incarnations of Buddha.
> [Aitken, *Encouraging Words*]

In other words, Torei Zenji is saying that everything is a manifestation of the enlightened heart-mind and that when our ancestors realized this, with their compassionate heart-minds they gave tender care to birds and beasts. At Maitreya Abbey in Berthoud, Colorado, where I am the abbess and one of the resident Zen teachers, we have lots of animals including horses, goats, chickens, a dog and a cat. They are rescued animals. We, teachers and residents, give tender care to them and when they get sick, we give them medicine and help them heal. The first time one of our hens got sick, we ran with her to a bird vet. The vet was amazed and said, "This is the first time I have seen someone bring a hen into my office." When one of our neighbors heard of us taking a chicken to the vet he said, "I always carry a first aid kit for chickens in my truck: a hatchet!" This is how country people deal with chickens when they get sick. How sad!

Torei Zenji goes on to say that when we realize the food, drink and clothing that nourish and protect us every day are none other than the enlightened heart-mind itself, we experience them as the warm skin and flesh of the great masters, the incarnate compassion of the Buddha.

I never had been able to sprout anything, although the idea has always been very appealing to me. Some instructions on how to sprout said that I had to buy jars with special lids. It seemed convoluted to me and I felt discouraged. However, while staying with my mother in Barcelona in February and March of 2019, and while I was finishing this book, I had been doing some cooking for her. I bought some whole green peas and I soaked them in water at night to cook them the next day. The next day I couldn't cook them because we went out to eat. Instead, I rinsed off the peas three times to prevent them from getting stinky. The following day, to my great surprise, I saw the peas starting to put out the beginnings of shoots. The peas were alive and they were opening to me!

At that moment I realized that the peas and everything else in this universe are no other than the enlightened heart-mind. I cannot explain why the experience of the peas sprouting was so enlightening to me. The koan collections are full of enlightenment stories of practitioners whose minds have become so still through the practice of zazen that they experienced in their own flesh the aliveness and interdependence of the whole universe with the sound of a pebble touching a bamboo branch, or at the shout of their teacher, or, like the Buddha, when seeing the morning star.

There is a koan in the *Mumonkan* that touches this matter, "Keitchu Makes Carts."

> Master Gettan said to a monk: "Keichu made a cart whose wheels had a hundred spokes. Take both front and rear parts away and remove the axle: then what will it be?" [Shibayama, *Zen Comments on the Mumonkan*, Case 8]

This koan is about realizing in yourself that not even the Buddha himself knows how the enlightened mind works. In order to answer this koan properly, one must be able to take a leap from the conceptual mind into the mind of emptiness. You learn to take that kind of leap in Zen training. It is like jumping off the constricting walls of the ego-mind into the freedom of a clean pool of crystalline waters made of blue sky, as wide and deep as the whole universe.

Torei Zenji continues:

> Even if someone turns against us and persecutes us with abusive language, we should bow down because that person is a merciful avatar of Buddha, trying to liberate us from the harmful karma that has been accumulated upon us from our own egotistic delusions and attachments through the countless cycles of karma.

This is how I feel about my aunt Titi now. She was a "merciful avatar of the Buddha, trying to liberate [me] from the harmful karma that had accumulated upon [me] from my own egotistic delusions and attachments through the countless cycles of karma." In this sentence, Torei Zenji describes in a poetic way the wondrous wisdom of the universe that, in accord with my own karma, manifested the drama with Titi which allowed me not only to know the purifying power of staying with my true feelings but also to enter into the Sambhogakaya realm when I witnessed the Lady of Light.

Torei Zenji concludes:

> Then on each moment's flash of our thought there will grow a lotus flower, and on each lotus flower will be revealed a Buddha. These Buddhas will glorify Sukhavati, the Pure Land, every moment and everywhere. May we extend this mind over all beings so that we and the world together may attain maturity in Buddha's wisdom.

Taking to heart the abusive language of Titi, I was able to enter into what is called in Buddhism the Sambhogakaya realm, the realm of light or heaven. To put it in Torei's words: "On each moment's flash of our thought there will grow a lotus flower, and on each lotus flower will be revealed a Buddha." At the end of the poem Torei Zenji wishes to extend the enlightened heart-mind to everyone in the world. This is called a return of merits. In Zen we always extend the merits of our practice and of our realizations to all beings everywhere.

Master Torei Zenji was a disciple of the Japanese Zen Master Hakuin. Master Hakuin lived in the seventeenth and eighteenth centuries and is considered to be the one who revitalized Zen, which was declining at that time. In Hakuin's autobiographical book, *Wild Ivy*, he shares his great childhood fear of hell, and how this fear motivated him in his spiritual path. When I first learned about Master Hakuin, I deeply connected with him and with my experience of fear, terror and hell. I thought to myself, "I am on the right path."

Hakuin wrote:

> There was in those days a priest of the Nichiren sect in Japan by the name of Nichigon Shonin.... Nichigon held a lecture-meeting.... I went with my mother, and we heard him describe in graphic detail the torments in each of the Eight Scorching Hells. He had every knee in the audience quaking, every liver in the house frozen stiff with fear. As little as I was, I was certainly no exception.
>
> When I went to bed that night, even in the security of my mother's bosom, my mind was in terrible turmoil. I lay awake sobbing miserably all night, my eyes swollen with tears. [Hakuin Ekaku, *Wild Ivy*]

Nichiren Buddhism developed in Japan in the thirteen century and emphasizes chanting the name of the *Lotus Sutra* as the main practice: *namu myoho renge kyo*. In this branch of Mahayana

Buddhism, proponents of Nichiren Buddhism believe that hell and heaven are states of one's consciousness, not a place in the underworld. The young Hakuin seemed to take the Nichiren priest's words literally, just like I did when Titi threatened me with the burning flames of hell.

After that event, Master Hakuin was very afraid of hell, and his fear was an important factor in his determination to later become a monk and follow the Zen path. Although it is customary in Japan to heat the water in soaking baths from a wood fire located under the bathtub, and Hakuin must have shared these baths from a very young age, the following incident illustrates with vivid detail his newly-gained terror of hell.

> I recall one particular occasion when my mother took me into the bath. She liked to have the water in the tub boiling hot. She wasn't happy unless the servant girl constantly stoked the fire with more and more wood and fanned it up into a blazing inferno. Flames would rush madly up and around, shooting out like angry waves. The water seethed and churned in the tub, making low, rumbling groans like thunder, striking a panic of terror into me. I let out howls of distress of such force they nearly burst the bamboo bands of the water buckets. [Hakuin Ekaku, *Wild Ivy*]

Like mine, Hakuin's spiritual life was powered by the fear he felt when he was a little boy. Like me also, Hakuin became a great devotee of *Kanzeon*, or *Kannon*, the bodhisattva of compassion. She is said to be able to appear in many different forms.

In Zen centers of Japanese origin, Kannon and Kanzeon representations are mostly female but sometimes they are male. In Sanskrit She is called Avalokitesvara and almost always is represented as a male. The same bodhisattva of compassion is called Kuan Yin or Guan Yin in China, where She always appears as a woman. I prefer the term Lady of Light because in my experience, She is the very essence of all of these deities.

The first time I saw a figure of Kannon or Kanzeon, it was a small wooden statue in a room off the zendo at the Rochester Zen Center. It reminded me of the Lady of Light. Prostrations and offerings were made to Her in this room. I was happily surprised and relieved that in the midst of so much harshness, the heart of love of the Lady of Light was there, even in the form of a small figurine. I did ask about her, but they told me that she was a man. To me she was a woman, but I didn't say any more because I was still locked in silence.

The Lady of Light emanated unconditional love. During my years of Zen training, I never heard a word about love. I remember one time during a question and answer period in a retreat with a teacher I shall call Sensei M, someone asked him how come love was never mentioned in Zen. Sensei M responded that love with capital "L" was the same as "Unmon's shit stick." Unmon was a Zen master during the golden age of Zen in T'ang Dynasty in China during the years 864-949 CE.

A monk asked Master Unmon, "What is Buddha?" Unmon answered, "A shit stick!" [Shibayama, *Zen Comments on the Mumonkan*, Case 21]

The monk in this koan was looking for an answer of holiness. When Unmon responds, "A shit stick!" he is saying that everything in the universe is not other than Buddha or the enlightened mind, even a shit stick. In Master Unmon's time, there was no such thing as toilet paper; people used sticks instead. Now, how did Sensei M compare love with a shit stick? This still remains a mystery to me.

There has not even been much talk in Zen about the heart, either. Our Zen liturgies come from the Japanese. In this language, mind and heart are the same character. This character has been translated to English as mind. I see this as a reason why Zen practice, in many cases, has become a mental practice.

Zen was born from the merging of Chinese Taoism and Indian Buddhism in the fifth century CE. Taoism was very fond of the female principle. The following poem from the *Tao Te Ching* by Lao Tzu is very significant, regarding the antiquity of the Great Mother religion and her connection to Zen practice.

The Tao is like a well:
Used but never used up.
It is like the eternal void:
Filled with infinite possibilities.
It is hidden but always present.
I don't know who gave birth to it.
It is older than God. [Chapter 4]

Lao Tzu continues:

The Tao is called the Great Mother:
Empty yet inexhaustible.
It gives words to infinite worlds.[Chapter 6]

In other words, since Zen was born from the merging of Chinese Taoism and Indian Buddhism and since the Tao is called the Great Mother, I believe that Zen was born from the merging of the religion of the Great Mother and Indian Buddhism.

When the Great Mother religion was persecuted, it went underground into the dark womb, resurfacing in India as Tantrism as explained later in this book. It makes perfect sense that it had also resurfaced in China as Taoism.

No wonder I had visions of the Great Mother through zazen practice. She has always been at the very heart of Zen's origins, then relegated to a figurine or a chant that in an abstract way was the symbol of compassion. We, the actual women who those figurines and chants represent, were not allowed in many Zen monasteries of China and Japan until the twentieth century. How sad!

The female bodhisattva of compassion Guan Yin looked a lot like the Lady of Light that I saw as a child. The resemblance of Guan Yin to the Virgin Mary is pretty astonishing, to the point that in many cases you cannot tell images or statues of them apart. Although I was never a devout Catholic as a child or young adult, I had always felt great connection to the Virgin Mary, ever since my father inadvertently identified what I saw as She. Since that time, I had thought that the name of the Lady of Light was the Virgin Mary.

The Virgin Mary, like the other deities I mentioned before – Kannon, Kanzeon, Avalokitesvara and Guan Yin – are all portrayed wearing long gowns and with similar faces that show their all-compassionate and loving hearts. These varied names are just different cultural labels, but to me all these deities are the Lady of Light. I thought it was kind of funny and it made me happy that She had so many different names. It was like encountering my relatives everywhere on a strange planet.

When I was 21 years old, at the end of a summer vacation in Puerto Rico, I was to return to Madrid in September. My mother was coming with me from Puerto Rico. We had to travel to New York and from there to Madrid. During the month prior to the trip, I started having terrible nightmares about the flight from New York to Madrid. I felt the plane was not going to make it across the Atlantic. It was a charter flight for students that my mother had found at a very good price. I begged and begged my mother to change the flight for another one with a different airline. But there was no way she would listen to me. Soon enough my mother and I were at Newark airport. We boarded the flight and took off. About 15 or 20 minutes later, we heard an explosion. One of the passengers yelled, "Fire! There's fire coming out one of the engines!" Then another explosion. The pilot ordered the flight attendants to sit down and put on their seat belts. We were going to try to go back to Newark. I looked at the faces of the flight attendants. They looked pretty tense and scared. Judging from their faces I thought that we were lost. My mother did not show a lot of emotion, but we held hands and I could tell she was scared too. I was praying to the Virgin Mary with all my might. I had forgotten myself in the prayer. There was only this prayer:

> Dios te salve María.
> Llena eres de gracia.
> El Señor es contigo.
> Bendita tu eres entre todas las mujeres. Y bendito es el fruto de tu vientre:
> Jesús.
> Santa María, Madre de Dios,

Ruega por nosotros pecadores, ahora y en la hora de nuestra muerte.
Amen.

Hail Mary full of Grace, the Lord is with thee.
Blessed are thou among women and blessed is the fruit of thy womb, Jesus.
Holy Mary Mother of God,
Pray for us sinners now and at the hour of our death.
Amen.

I learned the Hail Mary at the Catholic school I attended, in preparation for taking the First Communion. I didn't like the words very much in this prayer mostly for two reasons: first, it condemned sex by making the Virgin and the birth of Jesus into an immaculate conception; second, as the consequence of making the birth of Jesus into an immaculate conception, it made the rest of humankind into lesser beings.

The Hail Mary prayer talks about Mary being blessed among all the other women. My experience is that people of all genders are as blessed as Mary. She represents the deeper self of every person of every gender. My opinion is that the immaculate conception is another patriarchal manipulation to make women's free choice to sexuality into a sin and to make Jesus and Mary into something special, making them unattainable, not-human beings. In accord with my experience, having a baby with blood and pain is as immaculate a conception as any other. What is this interest of the old patriarchs to make us into what we are not? Is it that frightening to those men to see us soar, to unfold our wings and to explore our beings without limits and boundaries?

I saw the Lady of Light after I was told I was going to hell for having done something that my aunt considered sexual and bad. The Lady of Light I saw didn't have any concerns about sexuality. She was all goodness. There were no judgments of any kind in Her mind. This was a moment of transmission, although She did not speak a word. It is good that in Zen we teach about mind-to-mind transmission, or otherwise I would have been lost. My favorite koan about transmission is "Shakyamuni Buddha holds up a flower." The Buddha Shakyamuni holds up a flower, only the monk Mahakasyapa smiles. The other monks are at a loss. This episode represents the first transmission in Zen. The shared experience of an eternal moment united the minds of Mahakasyapa and Shakyamuni Buddha forever as one. The flower smiled! [Shibayama, *Zen Comments on the Mumonkan*, Case 6]

The union of two beings in sexual embrace is one of the most sacred things in life. How different it would have been if we had been told that Mary and Joseph fell terribly in love. That love was consummated in sacred sexual intercourse of unimaginable bliss. Out of that love, Jesus was born like many other people. Jesus wasn't special either.

I couldn't believe my eyes when I got to a poem in a koan that read, "If you find a Buddha, kill him!" This of course was not meant to be literal. It means not to look for a savior outside of us. It is impossible for me not to love Zen!

According to the Bodhisattvas' stages as described in the *Avatamsaka Sutra*, the fourth, fifth and sixth stages are world-transcending positions. The sutra says that the transcendent bodhisattvas are highly enlightened beings who have transcended this world, endowed with the ability to act beyond natural laws in ways that might not be obvious to the conventional eye.

When I prayed to Mary that day on the airplane, I did not put my attention in the meaning of the words in the prayer. My attention was in my heart. I prayed from my heart. The sounds of the words in this prayer created an energy in which I could forget myself and directly connect with the beautiful Lady of Light. I felt Her presence in my heart. I felt acceptance and unconditional love. My praying was a call of love. The answering was also a call of love. The airplane was able to land safely. Whew! I could not claim that the airplane landed safely because of my selfless praying but it did not matter either. What was important for me was that we were all safe, but most of all that I had connected again with the Lady of Light through the prayer of the Virgin Mary.

The sounds used to call in the Goddesses of the elements as described in Part Two of this book have no obvious meaning. They are primordial sounds. *Merriam-Webster* defines primordial as "existing at or since the beginning of the world or the universe." It is very useful that words have meaning, and it is wonderful that there are primordial sounds without meaning. They carry energy. Although the Hail Mary had meaning, I had connected to the sounds of it beyond the meaning.

The first time I found a chant in the Zen chanting book of primordial sounds, I was very intrigued by it. It is called, "Dharani to Prevent Disasters." A *dharani* is a mnemonic incantation, transliterated (often idiosyncratically) from Sanskrit. To put it another way: the words are not meaningless; they are derived from Sanskrit. There are many dharanis and mantras where the original can be deciphered, but the power of dharanis does not lie in an intellectual understanding of them as a literal text. We chant it from the *hara*, the belly, using very deep sounds:

No Mo San Man Da Moto Nan Oha Ra Chi Koto Sha Sono Nan To Ji To
En Gya Gya Gya Ki Gya Ki Un Nun Shiu Ra Shiu Ra Hara Shiu Ra Hara
Shiu Ra Chishu Sa Chishu Sa Chishu Ri Chishu Ri Sowa Ja Sowa Ja Sen
Chi Gya Shiri Ei So Mo Ko

When we don't focus on discovering literal meaning, the sounds connect us with universal energy. Through sound we can connect with that which does not die in us or in the universe. When we add visualization to sound, we become creators. The Goddess Practices are about creating health, wisdom and love in us and in the world, as described in Part Two of this book.

5

The Three Bodies of Buddha

During my school years when I was attending Las Reverendas Madres Irlandesas, which translates to The Reverend Irish Mothers, we had to memorize the catechism. I didn't like that we couldn't ask questions and that nothing was explained to us. I was so delighted years later when I heard that Zen was about our own individual experience and that we did not have to believe in anything that we had not experienced on our own. I thought to myself, "I can do this. I have been waiting for an opportunity to plunge thoroughly into my own experience all of my life."

Mostly, my Zen practice was about practicing zazen and penetrating into the non-duality of the depth of my own mind. During retreats the teacher might comment on one of the sutras or illustrate a koan from one of the koan collections. It was during a dharma talk while I was participating in a retreat in the Kapleau lineage that I first heard about the Buddhist doctrine of Trikaya. According to this doctrine a Buddha has three bodies, called *Dharmakaya*, *Sambhogakaya*, and *Nirmanakaya*. Very simply said, the Dharmakaya is the body of the absolute, the body of emptiness, beyond existence and non-existence. It is formless. The Nirmanakaya is the physical body that lives and dies. The Sambhogakaya is the realm of the light, or Buddha fields. It refers also to the subtle body of limitless form, the enjoyment body or clear light manifestations. A Buddha can appear in an enjoyment-body or clear light manifestation to teach bodhisattvas through visionary experiences.

We can say that our one body, like the Buddha's, has three different dimensions to it. As we get deeper in the practice of zazen meditation, we start experiencing and becoming more familiar with these three dimensions of our one body. The doctrine of Trikaya is different from the Catholic catechism. It lays out a path for Buddhist practitioners to experience and to understand what they experience. It is not something that the practitioner has to memorize or faithfully believe. The teachings of the three bodies of Buddha was very important to me, as they shed light into the nature of my own visionary experiences and the clear light manifestations I had.

Trinley Norbu Rinpoche, a contemporary teacher in the *Nyingma* school of Tibetan Buddhism, says:

In the Tantra, countless objects of refuge appear spontaneously out of one essential wisdom. Arising from wisdom as its reflection, all of these forms are Nirmanakaya. These forms can appear pure or impure according to the pattern of belief of the individual perceiving them.
[Trinley Norbu Rinpoche, forward to Dowman, *Sky Dancer: The Secret Life and Songs of the Lady Yeshe Tsogyel*]

In other words, the Nirmanakaya, the world of our ordinary perception, only appears ordinary due to our own cloudiness of mind, but in essence, the Nirmanakaya is not different from the Sambhogakaya, which is a pure, non-dual realm that only the non-dual being can perceive.

In *Genjokoan*, the thirteenth century Zen Master Dogen wrote:

To study the Buddha way is to study the self.
To study the self is to forget the self.
To forget the self
Is to be enlightened by the ten thousand dharmas.
To be enlightened by the ten thousand dharmas
Is to free one's body and mind and those of others.
No trace of enlightenment remains,
And this traceless enlightenment is continued forever.
[Maezumi, *The Way of Everyday Life*]

The "ten thousand dharmas" is another way of saying "all phenomena." To say, "To be enlightened by the ten thousand dharmas" is just another way to say, "countless objects of refuge appear spontaneously out of one essential wisdom." Through zazen meditation, we can open up our body and heart-mind and experience all things without attaching conceptual overlays to them. When we can do this, the Nirmanakaya is no other than the Buddha land of the Sambhogakaya.

Not attaching conceptual meaning to things is easier to do when we are in a seven-day Zen retreat, but more difficult to do when we are out of retreat. Out of retreat, our lives depend many times on attaching meaning to the events in our lives. I have seen how my first perception of things is sometimes a pure perception and is amazingly bright and beautiful. But quickly I have seen how my mind glues some meaning to whatever it is, depending on my archives of conditioning and my shadow. It is like wearing dirty glasses all the time. I have experienced also how the universe has its own currents, causes and conditions that I experience as winds connected with our specific karma. "Arising from wisdom as its reflections, all of these forms are Nirmanakaya. These forms can appear pure or impure according to the pattern of belief of the individual perceiving them."

It is very important to practice zazen meditation in order to have as clear a mind as possible, so that we can see the winds of karma for what they are. If our glasses of conditioning are cleaner, we can use the winds of karma to fly like birds, or *planear como los pájaros*, using these currents that come from the universe or the one essential wisdom. In order to do this, we shouldn't be too attached to our own agendas, otherwise we might get angry and fight hard when the universal winds do not conform to our ego will.

In the *Tao Te Ching*, Lao Tzu describes how the master, the enlightened person, rides the winds that come from the universe. The Master could be any gender, since the Chinese language doesn't make that distinction.

> Things arise and she lets them come;
> things disappear and she lets them go.
> She has but doesn't possess,
> acts but doesn't expect.
> When her work is done, she forgets it.
> That is why it lasts forever. [Chapter 2]

Winds bring change and we could say that anything that brings change is a wind from the universe. In other words, the Nirmanakaya, the world of our ordinary perception, only appears ordinary due to the cloudiness of mind of the individuals perceiving it.

We never know what the winds of change will bring, as illustrated by the Taoist story of the old, wise farmer and his horse:

> There was an old farmer who had worked his crops for many years. One day his horse ran away. Upon hearing the news, his neighbors came to visit. "Such bad luck," they said sympathetically. "Could be," the farmer replied.
>
> The next morning the horse returned, bringing with it another horse. "How wonderful," the neighbors exclaimed. "Could be," replied the old man.
>
> The following day, his son was plowing the field with the new horse, had an accident, and broke his leg. The neighbors again came to offer their sympathy on his misfortune. "Could be," answered the farmer.
>
> The day after, military officials came to the village to draft young men into the army. Seeing that the son's leg was broken, they passed him by. The neighbors congratulated the farmer on how well things had turned out. "Could be," said the farmer. And so it goes.
> [Watts, *Tao: The Watercourse Way*]

Norbu Rinpoche continues:

> Dharmakaya is the stainless space constantly pervading the sublime awareness of the Sambhogakaya and the ordinary, individual perceptions of the Nirmanakaya.

In other words, the Dharmakaya is the intrinsic essence of the Sambhogakaya and the Nirmanakaya. The Dharmakaya is at the heart of both. Zen discipline focuses greatly on the experience of the Dharmakaya. We call it emptiness. Emptiness cannot be known by the ordinary dualistic mind. In Zen we use koans as an aid to help the practitioners traverse safely through the intricate labyrinth of the dualistic mind and to experience emptiness.

This word emptiness is confusing to many people and can create misunderstandings. I like how it is described in Tibetan Buddhism as formless clear light. I view emptiness as clear light infused with full potentiality. This is difficult to explain. Only someone who has had the experience of emptiness can truly understand. Emptiness is the luminosity of the sky, the luminosity of the space element. Everything arises from emptiness and returns to emptiness, to space. Advanced practitioners can experience emptiness as unconditional love that fills even the deepest cells in their bodies, the deepest chambers of their hearts.

Someone asked me how the doctrine of Trikaya compares to the doctrine of the Holy Trinity. The Christian doctrine of the Trinity holds that God is one God, but three co-eternal essences – the Father, the Son (Jesus Christ), and the Holy Spirit – as one God in three Divine Persons. The Dharmakaya, the Realm of Emptiness, could be compared to God. Nirmanakaya, the realm of the human beings, could be said to refer to Jesus. The Sambhogakaya could be compared to the Holy Spirit, the realm of the light, heaven.

In Christianity the white dove symbolizes the Holy Spirit. On January 31, 2019, I am writing these lines while on the Spanish high-speed train called the *AVE*, or BIRD in English. I am travelling from Barcelona, where I've been helping my mother who has been sick, to Madrid, where I will be leading a *Zen from the Heart* Retreat. There are lots of pigeons in Barcelona city. They are starving. Every morning I walked around the Gothic City feeding the pigeons. They are very innocent and vulnerable – no wonder they represent the realm of heaven.

At home in Colorado I have chickens. They are also very vulnerable and innocent. How many chickens are in cruel conditions of exploitation everyday all over the world? I love my chickens. Sometimes they get sick and I have to bring them inside the house. Bringing a chicken back to health gives me an opportunity to surrender to compassionate action. The dove, the pigeon and the chicken all represent the very deep essence of the enlightened heart, so tender, innocent and vulnerable.

In Zen we have the koan, "How do you show an immovable tree in the high wind?" Most people think of an immovable tree to be the one that resists most against the wind. When

Zen students work with this koan, they present a very robust and stiff tree. That's not it. In Zen, an immovable tree in the high wind is the tree that moves with the wind, the tree that is flexible and vulnerable, bending in every direction and not offering any resistance to the wind. The unmovable tree is the tree that is one with the wind. This means that there is no energetic distinction between the tree and the wind. We could say the same thing about ourselves: the strongest person is the person who does not offer resistance to the winds of the universe, the person with a tender heart that is vulnerable to feel and to let go. This makes a person extremely strong.

The Sambhogakaya refers also to "the luminous form of clear light that a Buddhist practitioner attains upon reaching the highest dimensions of practice." This definition of the Sambhogakaya from Wikipedia is congruent with my experience. Looking back on the time Titi threatened me with the burning flames of hell, I understand that with the purity of innocence of a little girl, completely surrendering without any resistance to the feelings of the intense fear and terror I was experiencing, I was able as a child to transcend ordinary reality and enter into the realm of light, the Sambhogakaya.

I had other experiences of a realm beyond the ordinary. On several occasions throughout my life I've experienced time as non-linear. One evening when I was about 27 years old, I went running with a girl friend at a park in San Juan, Puerto Rico. During our run, a group of five or six men approached us and grabbed us by the arms. My first thought was that we were in big trouble. I looked around and I saw no passersby. Next to us there were some bushes and I thought they were going to push us in there and rape and kill us. Then in an instant everything became still, as though I had stepped out of time. I recognize the "out of time" episodes as out of time after they have passed. When they happen, time stops, everything stops; there are no sounds at all, only vast silence. There are no feelings either, only clarity. It was with great clarity that my heart opened up and I felt connected with the heart of the leader. Then I said, "I am Puerto Rican too." Then the leader said to the rest of the band, "Let them go."

I couldn't explain at the moment what had happened. I was just so grateful to be alive. However, later on, when I started practicing Zen and had entered moments of great clarity and openness of heart that were also outside of linear time, I realized that on that occasion I had connected with my future self – the self that deeply practiced the way of wisdom and compassion. Then I understood that my experience of seeing the Lady of Light when I was a girl was another instance in which I had contacted my future body of practice.

According to the Tibetan Buddhist tradition, those skilled in meditation, such as advanced lamas and yogis, as well as other highly realized Buddhists, may gain access to the Sambhogakaya and receive direct transmission of teachings.

I received direct transmission of teachings from the Lady of Light when I was only five-and-a-half years old. This transmission was both a sudden experience and a slow dawning of its immensity throughout my life. The sudden transmission was a transmission of unconditional love and innocence. The unfolding of the immensity of the transmission has rippled through all of my life in the form of messages, visions, insights and guiding dreams, which provided me with what seemed like a flashlight in the dark night.

However, the greatest help in fully understanding the visitation of the Lady of Light has been choosing to become openly vulnerable and to transform the poisonous energies of pride, anger, attachment, envy and fear in my own heart. First the practice of the Great Heart Way and then the practice of each elemental Goddess helped me to transform these poisons. When this happened, I realized that the Lady of Light had come from the depth of my own heart. Where else could She have come from? The puzzle was completed. The Goddess Practices were the last piece.

Some could say that the Lady of Light could have been an external being, a "divine" being that came to visit me. I could probably have believed that, if it had not been for the message I received the day after I saw her, as I mentioned earlier. As a girl of five-and-a-half, my first impression was that the Lady of Light was a visitation from a "holy being" outside of me. However, the messages, "You will understand later when you are old" and "It is okay to forget about this for now" turned out to be my life quest.

After leading a retreat in Madrid a few years ago, I went to visit the old house where I grew up with my family after we relocated to Madrid. As I looked at the house, I had a spontaneous visualization of all the Goddesses of the elements: yellow, blue, red, green and white surrounding the house and protecting me in my childhood. It was a very beautiful experience. I wondered if this happened because I had loosened my grasp on the ego-self reality a bit?

When I was studying with one of my later teachers, Pat Hawk Roshi, we were discussing a koan called "Nansen's Peony." In this koan a monk asked Master Nansen the meaning of the following phrase:

> Heaven and earth have the same root. The ten thousand things are one body.
> Nansen pointed to a peony and said: 'People these days see this flower as if in
> a dream.' [Wick, *Book of Equanimity*, Case 91]

Pat Hawk Roshi said that seeing things as if in a dream was a deep state of mind, a high state of awakening, of enlightenment. In order to see things as if in a dream, we already must have had an experience of the non-solidity of things. And although one sees life as a passing dream, one engages in this dream fully, with awareness and clarity. In Zen we use the phrase "Wake up!" a lot. At some point in our Zen practice, we wake up from the dream that our thoughts are real and we see them for what they are, a passing dream. However, being lost in thoughts is also called being in a dream. When we are lost in a dream, we have no awareness that it is a dream. This is a state of delusion. Wake up!

The Buddha said it this way:

> So you should think of all this fleeting world:
> A star at dawn, a bubble in a stream,
> A flash of lightening in a summer cloud,
> A flickering lamp, a phantom, and a dream.
> [Price and Mou-Lam, *The Diamond Sutra and the Sutra of Hui Neng*]

I say that seeing things as in a fairy tale is also a deep state of mind. However, seeing things as in a fairy tale and believing in fairy tales are two very different things. The first one is a state of enlightenment; the second, a state of delusion.

I was recently leading a Great Heart retreat in the outskirts of Madrid. A nice lady with beautiful energy, Aura, told the group her story. She lived as a child in a beautiful Spanish house with great open hallways and an inner courtyard. When Aura was little, she would run through the corridors, cross the courtyard and open the very large double wooden doors at the entrance. She was very happy in her magical world, full of extraordinary and imaginary friends. Next door to her house lived her uncle Pedro and her aunt Paula whom she loved. One day, Aura's mother told her that she was a liar, taking for granted that her imaginary friends were a lie. Aura's happy world collapsed.

As if this was not enough, her uncle Pedro died. Aura's mother told her that she had to go and sleep in bed with the widow Aunt Paula so that her aunt would not feel alone. Aura felt she was taking the place of the dead uncle. As you can imagine, this event marked the life of Aura, and the memory came out from Aura's unconscious mind during the retreat.

Aura healed this image by visualizing herself as a child and telling her mother, "Sorry, mum, but I am only a child and I cannot make my aunt happy by taking the place in my uncle's bed." She also visualized herself going to Aunt Paula when the latter was already in bed and giving her a good night kiss, then covering her with the blankets and leaving the room.

When I heard Aura telling her story, I lit up inside. "Aura's story is another fairy tale," I thought. I could see the happy and innocent Aura being plentiful in her wondrous house. Her mother taking the place of the bad witch, like my aunt did for me, destroyed the world of innocence. Aura now, as an adult, has to reclaim her mind of innocence and her magical world. When we are young, we bring to this world specific gifts that are intimately connected with our true self and our mission on this planet. When some of those aspects are shut down by the adults, they can't grow and develop with the rest of the personality and therefore we might feel as adults as if something is missing. Shishin Roshi and I talk more about this in *The Great Heart Way*. Aura is the grown-up heroine who descends into the darkness of her own unconscious mind to save little Aura from the fangs of the shadows.

6

The Path of the Heart

*I*t was my surrendering whole-heartedly into the experience of terror that allowed me to enter into the Sambhogakaya realm when I was a young child. My trust in the innate wisdom of my body to tap the power inherent in staying present with my true feelings formed the basis for the book *The Great Heart Way*, which I created later with my partner, Shishin Roshi.

However, in *The Great Heart Way* I was not able to explain completely my real reason for writing that book. I was not able to say that staying with my feelings of fear and terror as a child had taken me to the experience of a heavenly realm. I was still locked in silence. When I was little and I saw the Lady of Light, I heard a voice inside myself saying that I was going to understand when I was old. It was a bit like a prophecy. It was not time yet for me to speak up completely. I had to become old, old, first. The first time I truly saw my old face was less than two years ago. When I saw my face in the mirror, I suddenly recognized that I was old. I was so happy singing to myself, "I'm old, I'm old." My whole life I've been waiting for this moment of being old in order to understand my childhood prophecy. This reminded me of one of the poems from the Five Ranks of Zen Master Tozan. Tozan was a notable Zen master of the ninth century in China. His poem encapsulates my Zen journey and experience.

> An old crone, having just awakened, comes upon an ancient mirror
> And clearly sees a face that is no other than her own.
> Don't lose sight of your face again and go chasing your shadows.
> [Powell, *Record of Tung-Shan*]

I trained in the Zen lineage of Philip Kapleau for about eight years, from 1986 to 1994. After eight years, I felt I was done with the almost abusive rigidity of the Zen training of the Kapleau lineage as it was then. I switched to the lineage of Aitken Roshi, also a Soto and Rinzai lineage. I studied for about four more years, from 1994 to 1998, with Pat Hawk Roshi, a successor of Aitken Roshi. It was very soothing for me to meet with a kind Zen teacher like

Pat Hawk Roshi, and I practiced with him almost to the end of my Zen studies. I used to travel monthly to Amarillo, Texas, to participate with him in retreats of four to seven days.

Pat Hawk Roshi was also a Catholic Priest. In the Christian retreat center where he resided, he was allowed his own Zen area. At other Zen centers I had become used to sleeping in large dorms and sharing bathrooms. But in Pat Hawk's place we could have our own individual rooms with private bathrooms. This was a luxury to me, and it did not cost any more than the other retreat centers where I had been practicing. The retreat center was surrounded by empty fields owned by the church. It felt like being in the countryside.

On the sixth night of a seven-day retreat, in the year 2000 when I was at a retreat with Pat Hawk Roshi, I came to my room and, without turning the lights on, I sat in a comfortable chair to enjoy the empty clarity of my mind as the night light shone through the tall rectangular window. Absorbed in this clarity, I felt the presence of a spirit of light. I didn't see it; I only felt its transparent and divine presence. And this spirit presented me with two paths: one was the path of the heart and the other the path of the samurai. With all the hard Zen training that I had received before Pat Hawk, I had become a samurai woman. I felt very strong and powerful being able to cut through all of my feelings without hesitation. But now, I clearly saw in my mind the image of coming to a fork in my spiritual path. I had to choose between the path of the heart and the path of the samurai. After contemplating both paths for an instant, I chose the path of the heart. The very moment I made my selection, it was as if an ancient and vast dam had opened that had been holding back a tremendous reservoir of pain. It was not personal pain that I felt, it was the collective pain of the whole world. That night I cried what I call "rivers and lakes." I wasn't crying for any particular reason; it was just like a torrential rain in the rainforest. It was as if the Earth was releasing some of her suffering through me.

That was not the first time I felt a deep connection to the Earth. When I was seven years old, I used to spend weekends and vacations at the house we had on the beach outside San Juan. I spent many hours in the ocean. One time I got into the bad habit of killing sea urchins. Although the entrance into the water was sandy, if I swam some distance I would get to a place where the seaweed was dense. I actually had to take a step up to stand on the seaweed. I got the idea of bringing my rubber boots. I would wade through the water carrying the boots to the seaweed area, then put on the boots to stand on the seaweed. This area was a few feet above the sandy area, so when I stood up on it, the water was below my waist. The water was always so clear and transparent. Standing up I could see from above all the white urchins hiding among the seaweed. Then I would crunch them under my boots. It was a pleasure for me to feel this crunch. One day, as I placed one foot to climb to the seaweed area, I felt the Earth's heart beating through the bottom of my boot. The Earth's beating was so strong and clear that I was paralyzed for a while. I went back to the shore and never again killed a sea urchin.

That night at Pat Hawk's retreat, after crying torrents of tears and before going to bed, I looked out the window and I saw that my eyes were the shining stars. There were lots of them.

My mind had gotten so big and my heart so expanded that I had a clear revelation that the stars were actually my own eyes looking at my eyes. There was no separation between my eyes and the stars. My eyes were the stars and the stars were my eyes. I went to sleep with a very tender and soothing feeling in my heart. I felt loved by the universe. There is a verse in case 47 of the *Mumonkan*, which always connects me with this experience. Here the word *kalpa* is used to express infinite time.

> This one instant as it is, is an infinite number of kalpas.
> An infinite number of kalpas is at the same time this one instant.
> If you see into this fact,
> The True self which is seeing has been seen into.
> [Shibayama, *Zen Comments on the Mumonkan*, Case 47]

As I lay down, I entered into a different dimension. It was again the Sambhogakaya dimension. I had been there before when I was a young child and I recognized it. In this dimension there is no suffering, only great love, and everything seems to be tinted with a soft blue light. And in that dimension, I manifested as a woman of light myself and every form of life came out of my womb, even the small insects. I had become the same woman of light that had come to visit me when I was five-and-a-half. Standing behind me there was a man of light. I later recognized this man as the essence of Shishin Roshi, whom I had not met yet.

In the morning, I happily went to tell my experience to Pat Hawk Roshi. He had always been so kind to me but this time he wasn't. My koan studies with him were almost completed and I had a promising future as his successor. He wasn't in the least bit happy when I told him that I had become a woman of light and that everything had come from my womb. He looked serious and kind of upset. Then he told me that if I wanted to continue with my Zen career, I had to forget about that experience. This is all he said. He didn't explain at all. I was shocked to hear this.

"Forget about that experience?" I replied. "How could I forget about that experience? How could I betray my own heart? That is impossible!"

I went to my room, packed up all of my things, threw them in the back of my Pathfinder and left the retreat. I had so many tears, I could hardly see the road and I had to drive nine hours to get back home. I stopped in the first post office I found. I wrote the following poem and sent it to my teacher in an express envelope:

> From the dimension of blue light,
> Not even a thousand steel swords can kill me,
> Free from life and death,
> My tears make the shining stars;

And my laughter, the ocean dance,
I'm not a Buddha though,
But the Mother of All Things.

Once again, I had entered the Sambhogakaya realm, but this time I felt that I myself had become a Woman of Light, the Sacred Feminine, the Great Mother. And from Her, from my womb, every creature emanated. I also realized that we, all women, are endowed with the potential to experience this.

Once I had this experience, it was impossible to forget about it. I had so many questions. Why was my teacher so upset because I had an experience like that of the Sacred Feminine? Shouldn't he be happy for me instead? Later on, it became clear to me that I had triggered my teacher, who was also a Catholic priest and was probably conditioned by the same system of the patriarchal priests of ancient times that believed in a male God who commanded women to be obedient to men.

Last year I mentioned this story as part of a Dharma talk I was giving at Great Mountain Zen Center, and during the question and answer period someone asked me if Pat Hawk Roshi, when he said that I had to forget about my experience, just meant that I should let go of it? I replied that Pat Hawk didn't just say that I had to forget about my experience, he said that if I wanted to continue with my Zen career, I had to forget about that experience. I explained that when my teacher had said this to me, his tone was not amicable – it was a threat and a command.

It is true, however, that in Zen in order to continue moving deeper into the emptiness of our minds, we need to let go of our enlightenment experiences. This is very important. A few months before my break with my teacher happened, I had another extraordinary experience. I had returned home from another seven-day retreat in Amarillo. The next day I went to pick up my kids from school and a policeman with a radar gun stopped me for driving above the speed limit. The image of seeing that policeman pointing at me with what resembled a regular gun struck me deeply. Coming from a seven-day retreat, I was open and raw. When I arrived home, I went to my studio and I noticed the beautiful clear light that came through the windows. Then I had a vision of myself in what seemed like the French Revolution. There were lots of people rebelling around a large plaza. I was tied up on a large wooden stand at the center of the plaza together with other people. We were going to be decapitated and my turn was next. I approached the wooden pillar. I placed my head down. The person with a black hood covering his head raised the guillotine up and whoosh! At that very moment, and with all the intensity I had accumulated during the seven-day retreat, I asked myself as I saw my dead head rolling down, "And now, what? Now, what?"

Then, at the very moment I finished asking those questions something unimaginable happened. My physical body in the room turned into a spinning vortex of light. It happened in an instant. I saw my body dissolving into this vortex, starting with my lower body. I cannot say that I saw this with my physical eyes because I did not have any. I perceived everything with the eyes of consciousness while at the same time I was consciousness itself. I became the consciousness of the sky, clouds, grasses and the house. Everything was perfectly harmonious. There were no thoughts, no mind, no fear. I was only consciousness, awareness without a physical body. I do not know how long this lasted but after some time I became again a vortex of light that, entering through the closed window of my studio, formed my body again.

I was mute in awe from what had just happened. When my ego mind returned, I asked myself, "What was that? What was that?" This experience was not part of the enlightenment experiences I had read about in Philip Kapleau's book, *The Three Pillars of Zen*! What was that?

I mentioned my experience to a fellow practitioner, and he thought that I had had a hallucination, or makyo as it is called in Zen. I had lots of makyos when I first practiced Zen. Makyos are products of the ego-mind that you can control by not paying attention to them. During one of the firsts seven-day retreats I attended at the Rochester Zen Center, I was trapped by makyos. We used to sit in zazen looking at a white wall. In this wall my mind projected many different forms and shapes. I was mesmerized by this phenomenon in spite of all the warnings the teacher and the monitors had given us.

I knew that what had just happened to me was not a makyo, nor a product of the ego mind; I did not have a mind at all. I did not have a physical body either except for the grasses, the sky, the house and the clouds.

When I went to the next retreat in Amarillo, I told Pat Hawk what had happened, and he remained silent. Then I said, "Please tell me what it was. My friend says it was a makyo, but I know it wasn't." I begged again, "You have to tell me what it was." Then Pat Hawk Roshi said, "It was a satori." In the lineage of Philip Kapleau as well as in the lineage of Pat Hawk Roshi, they use two different categories to distinguish the degree of enlightenment experiences. They use the term kensho for a small experience and satori for a large experience. When Pat Hawk replied, "It was a satori." I said, "Oh, a small satori." "No," he said, "a large one!" Oh! I was mute again. It was interesting that in this case Pat Hawk did not say that I had to forget about that experience. Reflecting on this now, as I write these pages, I can only guess that the experience of a woman giving birth to all creation must have disturbed Pat Hawk's beliefs in Christian theology. He had to reject my experience. However, that experience for me was stronger than the experience of my physical dissolution in a vortex of light. I couldn't forget about it. I could not let go of it before having someone confirm it first, like he had just done with my satori experience. These experiences do not make me feel proud or important or special; on the contrary they make me humble, unimportant and unspecial. Before now I have only shared these experiences with a handful of people.

7

The Dakini

A few years ago, I found the following description of the Sacred Feminine. The contemporary *Nyingma* teacher Trinley Norbu Rinpoche says,

In the profound [Tibetan Buddhist] sutra system, the Dakini is called the Great Mother.

> Indescribable, unimaginable Perfection of Wisdom, Unborn, un-
> obstructed essence of sky, She is sustained by self-awareness alone:
> I bow down before the great Mother of the Victorious Ones, past,
> present and future.

Thus it is written in the *Great Paramita Sutra*. In the precious tantric tradition, 'desireless, blissful wisdom is the essence of all desirable qualities, unobstructed going and coming in endless space.' This wisdom is called 'the Sky Dancer', feminine wisdom, the Dakini.
[Trinley Norbu Rinpoche, forward to Dowman, *Sky Dancer: The Secret Life and Songs of the Lady Yeshe Tsogyel*]

My teacher's rejection of my experience of being a Lady of Light helped me to release all the old feelings still trapped in my body since the first time I saw Her, when my experience was rejected by my family. When my teacher asked me to forget about my experience, I had the opportunity to make a new choice and stand with Her. I would not betray my soul in order to become a Zen teacher. I use the term soul as I expressed earlier to refer to the deepest essence of my heart, not in the way that Christians or Muslims might think of it: a permanent, unchanging essential nature that survives after death. The Lady of Light emanated from this deep place in my heart. First, I saw Her when I was a young girl; then I saw Her as I recounted in the previous chapter; and now this experience is available to me every time I visualize Her.

When I left the retreat, I thought I had put an end to my Zen career and, although this felt very right in my heart, it was also very painful. I had never practiced anything else besides Zen, but I was having experiences that were not common in the Zen traditions. It was my experience with all the teachers with whom I had trained, until I met Shishin Roshi, that they had, metaphorically speaking, a guidebook that was passed down from male to male. Women's experiences and insights were absent from this book. Those Zen teachers discarded anything that did not fit with their training or that was not part of their experience, understandably.

I knew without a bit of doubt that the experiences I was having were real. However, for my peace of mind, I needed to find someone who would understand what was happening to me. I needed to be confirmed.

At this point in my life, my two sons, Lucas and Roldán, were respectively twelve and six years old. The export/import business I had started with my second husband was doing very well and gave me the means to go on my quest, although my marriage had been falling apart for a few years then and we had separated. I visited a couple of Zen teachers. One of them I will call LN. She said that we could do some women's koans together. I agreed. I traveled to a retreat that she and two other teachers whom I will call RG and DS, were leading together. She said that she would bring a copy of the women's koans with her. I explained to her that it was expensive for me to pay for the retreat, to travel to California, and rent a car to get back from the retreat center to the airport. In addition to that, I explained to her that I had two small children and that I had to arrange for their care during my absence, so I would only make the journey to California in order to investigate these "special women's koans" that she was offering to me. I felt that we had an agreement, and since it was for a worthy cause, I went to the retreat.

There were lots and lots of people in that retreat. It was like nothing I had seen before. The retreat was taking place at a retreat center in the desert somewhere outside Palm Springs in a large old house that had two floors and a basement. Around this main building were other smaller houses with dorms and bathrooms. I never saw LN and RG sitting in the zendo with us, but we could hear their laughter through the cracks of the wooden floor in the zendo. It sounded like they were partying while we were sitting. They did come and give Dharma talks that were void of the aura of reverence and respect that sitting in silence gives to a Dharma talk.

Finally, it was my time to go to dokusan with LN. When I asked her about the women's koans she said, "I forgot to bring the women's koans." I felt so devastated inside, even betrayed, that I couldn't utter a word. She gave me another koan, but it was very simple. I was not really interested in any other koans and I doubted her insight.

The other two teachers were giving dokusan as well. Since LN was not true to her word and had made me waste my time and money by going there, I did not feel any loyalty to her and decided to try the other two teachers. I went with RG first. He was very nice in the first interview. He said that my experiences were part of my own mind. Yes, of course! This is something that Zen teachers say when they don't know what to say. Everything is part of our own mind. Even the whole universe is part of our mind. He said that I could come back and work with him on some koans. He also said that next time I could dodge the line by telling the monitor he had said so. There were huge lines to go to dokusan with him, so the prospect of being able to dodge the line seemed very appealing to me and I was curious about what koans he thought I could work with.

The next day I saw LN and RG talking to each other in the hallways of the retreat house. They seemed in distress and I had the thought I was the cause of their distress. I quickly discarded this idea as being the product of my own paranoia. From the very beginning of my arrival there, I had not felt welcomed except by then-Sensei [now Roshi] DS, who had given me a ride from Palm Springs to the Retreat Center. He was warm and truly welcoming.

When you are a beginner Zen student everyone loves you, but when you are a senior and you transfer to another sangha, some people, including teachers, might be suspicious of you and even afraid of your insight.

In Colorado, when I was studying at the Front Range Dharma Center, which at the time was led by Sensei M, successor of Philip Kapleau, I experienced his fear of my insight. I had been a very devoted student of his. There was a big scandal involving Philip Kapleau and it had all come out before I moved to Colorado. Philip Kapleau had studied Zen in Japan for several years with the very well-known Yasutani Roshi. Philip Kapleau went through the first two books of koans, if that much. Then he had to travel to the US and Yasutani Roshi gave him permission to give talks on Zen and start his own group. However, instead of that, Philip Kapleau empowered himself as a *Roshi*, the highest title a Zen teacher can have. Later Yasutani Roshi came to the US for a visit and found out that Kapleau had abused the power conferred on him. The result was that they broke their relationship. Kapleau had received huge amounts of money from donors to start the Zen Center in Rochester. He had to invent his own curriculum of Zen koans. In order to make up for the lack of his Zen koan studies that typically include five books and over 700 koans, Kapleau decided that his students should give two rounds of study to the only two books that seemed familiar to him.

I found out about this when I was studying with Kapleau in Florida, where he had relocated. I had started my second round on the first book of koans, the *Mumonkan*. Kapleau had gotten sick and Sensei M had come to visit him. Sensei M told us about all of this and invited me and my then-husband to come to Fort Collins, Colorado to study with him. He also told us that he would continue to study the other Zen books of koans with Robert Aitken Roshi.

Since Philip Kapleau had gotten very sick and was not seeing students anymore, we decided to move to the Colorado area. In the meantime, Sensei M had gone to Hawaii to study with Aitken Roshi, but Aitken had not accepted his understanding of the second book of koans, *The Blue Cliff Record*, and had made him repeat this book.

Suddenly, after I moved to Colorado, Sensei M's behavior made me wonder if perhaps he saw me as a threat because we were working on the same book of koans. I did not find out about this until later. I only knew that he tried to reject me in any possible way. He created a special Zen program to which I applied, but he wrote me a letter saying that he could not accept me because I lived in Boulder where, he said, only people as handsome as Robert Redford lived and that I would only come to Fort Collins to "pollute the city."

I later came to believe that he was afraid of me and that he wanted to slow down my koan study so that he could stay ahead of me. I remember during a retreat I had asked permission from the monitor to check on my kids by phone. It was a brief conversation. Later on that evening Sensei M said that it was the fault of a person talking on the phone that the retreat was falling apart. At the time, I never took anything he said personally; I thought he was teaching me out of the goodness of his heart in order to open up my ego. I took his teaching wholeheartedly without defending myself. It was only later, after a Dharma combat, that I saw his mask coming off in a way that suggested he felt threatened.

Dharma combat is a ceremony where students challenge their understanding of a koan against the understanding of the teacher. During one such Dharma combat, I wanted to show my teacher how much I had learned from him. So I went to the zendo and sat in zazen a couple of hours before anyone else. I had entered into a deep concentration, *samadhi*, by the time everyone arrived.

There must have been between 80 and 100 people in the room. The monitor announced the Dharma combat, read the koan to investigate, and struck the wooden block three times. I felt very expanded. Everyone in the audience was no other than myself. When the monitor announced the koan it was the koan Mu, asking "Does a dog have Buddha Nature or not?" I did not hesitate and jumped in front of the teacher's seat before anyone else. Whoever does not fall into dualism wins the Dharma combat.

"Do you want to know whether a dog has Buddha nature or not?" I asked him.

"Yes," he replied.

"Ask me," I said. I couldn't believe what happened next. The teacher fell apart. He became very nervous, looking at the audience and sweeping his gaze back and forth as if at a tennis match. He did not know what to do or say. Then after a while all he was able to come up with was to scold me, "You did not come here to expound this koan in front of everyone."

Me? I thought. I had just come to participate wholeheartedly in a Dharma combat and now he was saying that somehow his inadequacy was my fault?

He was getting more and more nervous looking at the audience as if he was in a theater where the performance had been a failure.

"You and I are going to finish this in private. A teacher could not allow a student to surpass him," he said.

In private? I thought. It was as if a veil had fallen from my eyes and I saw him for the first time for what he was – a fake. I have read how happy the Zen teachers from olden times were when a student surpassed them. That was a time of great celebration. But here at the Front

Range Dharma Center with Sensei M, it was a shame. It was after this unfortunate and painful event that I switched teachers to Pat Hawk Roshi.

Now, at the LN retreat, I was about to experience what seemed like a version of the same thing. I went to the front of the line for the next dokusan with RG, just as he had told me to, and talked to the monitor. The monitor told me that things had changed and that I had to go back to the end of the line. I did. I waited patiently for a long time for my turn. Finally, when my turn arrived, I went into the dokusan room and sat before him. He was not nice anymore. He was aggressive towards me. He pushed me back by my nose with his index finger while saying, "I do not teach students, I only teach teachers. I do not have any time for you."

Wow! After all, my paranoia was not paranoia, but reality. I had no idea what LN had told RG, but obviously it was not good.

During the rest of the retreat I went to dokusan with DS. He was very kind, a really compassionate human being. I couldn't tell him what had happen to me in that retreat because I didn't think there was any chance that he would believe me. I tried to do some koans with him, but my mind was not into it anymore. At the end of the retreat I was called to go see LN in dokusan. I went. Angrily she told me that I was a very dishonest person. I was baffled by her statement. She hardly knew me well enough to judge me. Nevertheless, I intuitively answered, "I am honest to myself!" She said, "That's the problem!" I bowed to her and left the room.

At the end of the retreat there was a ceremony in which LN started singing and dancing, spraying everyone with water from the tip of a fern branch. Fortunately, I was able to grab a sutra book and protect my head from her "blessings."

About six months after I had left my teacher Pat Hawk in 2000, I received a letter from a Zen group in Boulder announcing that a Zen master had moved to Boulder and that he was teaching at Naropa University. One day I went to meet this new Zen teacher, Sensei Gerry Shishin Wick, a successor of Maezumi Roshi, who would be empowered as a Roshi a few years later by Roshi Bernie Glassman.

When I told him about my experience of becoming a woman of light and giving birth to the world, he said, "I don't know what happened to you, but I do support you in your search of finding out what it is." His words were so soothing to me. I had found someone who would support me in my search. Not only that, I had found someone who was honest enough to say that he didn't understand, instead of rejecting me or making up something to say about it.

It was around that time that Lama Tsultrim Allione's book, *Women of Wisdom*, fortuitously fell into my hands. In the introduction to this book, she talked about the enlightenment experiences of some women. I recognized my experiences there. In the book, I found some contact information for Lama Tsultrim at Tara Mandala, her retreat center near Pagosa Springs, Colorado. I called and was happily surprised when she answered. I told her about my predicament, and she agreed to have an interview with me.

I traveled to Pagosa Springs with my six-year-old son, Roldán. The first afternoon we arrived there, we stayed in a motel and I took my son to the springs. The following day was the interview. Roldán came with me. When I arrived at the retreat center, a few people guided me to the interview place, outdoors under a canopy. When I saw Lama Tsultrim coming, I immediately felt at home. She had an aura of clear light around her. She was beautiful with a very serene and peaceful face. Her hair was a light color and she was wearing a long skirt with a loose blouse with long sleeves and a shawl, all in soft colors. While we talked, my son Roldán circumambulated both of us non-stop. Lama Tsultrim admired him and frequently glanced at him with a broad smile. When I was done telling her about my experiences she said, "You are having dakini experiences."

"Dakini?" I said. I had never heard this word before. I felt so happy that she knew the word for it. I felt so relieved that what had happened to me even had a name! Dakini! This word was like music to my ears. Lama Tsultrim didn't explain more and I did not ask any questions. Somehow, I knew instantly without words that dakini was a term used for en-lightened women. In her book *Women of Wisdom*, Lama Tsultrim tells stories of enlightened women of Tibet. I immediately felt connected to those women. Those women also, because they were different from the rest of society, had to endure lots of hardships and abuse. I felt I had been very lucky to meet a woman like Lama Tsultrim who knew a lot about women's experiences of the past and of the present.

8

The Sacred Feminine

When I came back to Boulder, I told Shishin Sensei, "I found out what happened to me. It's called dakini experiences!" He seemed not to be familiar with that word, so I explained, "Dakini is a term used in Tibetan Buddhism that refers to enlightened women." Now that I knew what had happened to me, I was able to let go of it and resume my Zen studies with Shishin Sensei at Great Mountain Zen Center. Once again, I participated in all the meditation sessions and in all the retreats that were offered. I had totally let go of my dakini experiences, and I continued entering deeper and deeper in the emptiness of my mind as if nothing had happened.

However, somehow now, things were different and entering into emptiness became the door to other realities. Emptiness is the vast inner space that exists before creation. It is very luminous. It is spacious luminosity. Through this inner space, clear memories of a history different from the one that had been told to us, and that I had learned in college, started to emanate. These memories appearing in my mind were of a benign sacred feminine that emanated unconditional love, clear and pure. She didn't instill fear or anger.

Recently, I read of a vision by Hildegard of Bingen, the twelfth-century German Christian mystic. She also heard a voice speaking inside her, and her description of a radiant Lady of Light was so similar to mine that it is almost as if she had had my experiences!

Hildegard says,

> I heard a voice speaking to me:
>
> The young woman who you see is Love…. She has her tent in eternity…. It was love which was the source of this creation in the beginning…. As though in the blinking of an eye, the whole creation was formed through love. The young woman is radiant in such a clear, lightning-like brilliance of countenance that you can't fully look at her…. She holds the sun and the moon in her right hand and embraces them tenderly…. The whole of creation call this maiden 'Lady'. For it was from her that all creation proceeded, since Love was the first. She

made everything…. Love was in eternity and brought forth, in the beginning of all holiness, all creatures without any admixture of evil. Adam and Eve, as well were produced by love from the pure nature of the Earth.
[Fox, *Hildegard of Bingen: A Saint of Our Times*]

Practicing zazen meditation we can enter through the many gates of emptiness, sometimes accessing the past and the future. Time, in actuality, always stands still; we think that time passes, but actually we are the ones that pass. We also think of the past as distant, but actually it is and it is not. Most people have a hard time understanding that although time is linear in the relative world, in the absolute reality time doesn't exist. However, through the experience of in-depth Zen practice, this can become perfectly clear. All of our previous experiences in this life and even into the distant past can be accessed through the gate of emptiness as easily as dipping a hand into a pool of water, for those who carry this particular karma.

There is a lot more to us than what we see. We usually identify ourselves with the part of us that is visible. But we are like trees. So much of the tree grows below the surface of the Earth. There is so much to us that exists underneath the ground – our collective history. The Earth keeps the memory of everything.

While finishing my Zen studies with Shishin Roshi, I dreamt of an ancient lady. She was naked. She was carrying ornaments made of shells. She had several hands that carried bones and conch shells. Beside her there was a stream. Above the stream there was a large wheel-shaped wooden sphere, which I knew in the dream to be a dharma wheel. Above all of these there were large roots, then dirt, and then a large and vast tree. It was clear that She was back and She was going to stay. In my dream the sacred feminine that had been suppressed and forced underground since the beginning of the Christian era was emerging now, in this current age, because we women are emerging and waking up too from the nightmare of patriarchy. She is the fierce Goddess of Compassion. The Earth had kept Her safe in her belly all of these years.

The following realization came to me years ago when I was sitting in zazen. I felt as if the ground had opened up and a spiral into the distant past had become accessible. It was as though a vortex of time lit up and the unbroken lineage of my ancestral line of spiritual women entered my body. The spirit of who we are at the personal and at the collective level is available to each one of us.

I remember the day that Shishin Roshi ordained me as a Zen priestess. It was on a Friday the thirteenth. We didn't choose that number; it was just a coincidence. Thirteen is an ancient sacred number. At the beginning of the ceremony when I was returning to my seat in front of the altar after doing my bows to the altar, I saw with my mind's eye many spirit women of red color with shadowy, ghostly shapes floating into the room, coming to join the ceremony with me. They entered the room from the side of the house that faced the open space with Waneka

Lake. I felt they were coming from the water and that the red color symbolized blood. I knew that they were my spiritual ancestors from time immemorial.

In the Zen tradition we have some koans relating to old women in ancient China who sold tea and cakes in huts near the monasteries. In contrast to the Zen masters who lived in the monasteries and whose names are well known to us, these old ladies have no names. They were usually very enlightened women who listened to the dharma on the rare occasions they were invited inside the Dharma Hall. They had a solitary practice for the most part because they weren't allowed to practice in the monasteries. My heart is always with these ladies. I feel oneness with them. When I was studying koans, I felt so identified with them, I was them and they were me. I was so desperate for the teachings I would have done the same as they did, serving tea and cakes near monasteries just to catch a few crumbs of the dharma. They are anonymous and nameless in the stories we tell about them today, and I do not want to invent fake names to give them.

There is a koan about an old lady of the Pure Land faith. She was walking along the road when she met a Zen master, who said to her,

> "On your way to the Pure Land, eh Granny?"
> She nodded.
> "Holy Amitabha's there, waiting for you, I expect."
> She shook her head.
> "Not there? The Buddha's not in the Pure Land? Where is he then?"
> She tapped twice over her heart and went on her way.
> The Zen Master opened his eyes wide in appreciation and said, "You are a real Pure Lander."
> [Caplow and Moon, *The Hidden Lamp*, Case 4]

In the Pure Land tradition of Buddhism, by praying to Amitabha Buddha, adherents believe that they will be reborn in the Pure Land where they will be enlightened and able to enter nirvana. Where is the Pure Land? This woman knew that it is right here in her heart. Where is Amitabha Buddha? Who is Amitabha Buddha? This woman knew where She was.

The lady in this koan did not yield to the insults of the Zen Master. She walked straight with her hand over her heart. Can we do that?

We remember the enlightened and nameless old ladies in our services at Great Mountain Zen Center during the dedication of the *Identity of Relative and Absolute* chant. After the list of male teachers honored in our dedication, we include, "And all women honored ones throughout history whose names have been forgotten or left unsaid."

On the day of my ordination, when the red spirit women entered and I recognized them as spiritual ancestors, I knew that these ancestors stretched back centuries and included the nameless wise tea ladies.

Even though when they first entered the room they floated and dispersed among the people seated for the ceremony, during the ceremony itself they stayed next to me. I was not afraid at all; on the contrary, I was very touched, moved, honored and humbled at the same time. The nameless women ancestors are my heart and they share my name. I felt it was a collective ceremony for all of us.

9

The Downfall of the Great Mother

Entering wholeheartedly into my personal karma through my zazen practice, I was able to open up to the feminine collective karma. It was then that I started to have memories of a distant past, a past different from the history that I had studied as an archaeologist in Spain. I had clear visions of the sacred feminine in Her Sambhogakaya body of light emanating unconditional love.

I had studied archaeology in Spain from 1972 to 1976 when the fascist dictator Francisco Franco was in power. Archeological evidence that contradicted Franco's politics and the teachings of the Catholic Church was veiled and kept secret at that time. Part of this deliberate veiling of information included party-line interpretations of artifacts recovered from digs located from Europe to the Middle East. Part of the reason for this was that the majority of the archaeological information and the religious history of antiquity was originally compiled by archaeologists, historians and theologians raised in Judeo-Christian societies who shared the same politico-religious view which was prevalent at that time. Consciously and unconsciously, they interpreted the archaeological data in order to conform with their own Judeo-Christian beliefs. Like researchers in many fields, the leading archeologists in the nineteenth and twentieth centuries saw what they were trained to see through the filter of their preconceived notions, rather than looking at the archeological data with fresh eyes and unbiased views.

More recently, experts have drawn different conclusions. One example is Professor Marija Gimbutas through her detailed evaluations of archaeological artifacts excavated over the entirety of Europe, the Middle East and India dating from the Paleolithic and Neolithic eras. Another is Professor Elaine Pagels, whose work draws from translations of the Gnostic Gospels in the Nag Hammadi scrolls discovered in Egypt. Many other scholars support their work. They agree with Gimbutas that:

> During the Paleolithic and Neolithic eras of prehistory, the worship of a female deity as the creatress of life mirrors the matrilineal or mother-kinship system that most likely existed at that time (in Old Europe). ...the father

image so prevalent in later times, is missing. The Goddess is nature and earth itself, pulsating with the seasons, bringing life in spring and death in winter. She also represents continuity of life as a perpetual regenerator, protectress and nourisher. [Gimbutas, *The Living Goddess*]

These conclusions are supported by excavations ranging from Scandinavia and the British Isles, through Southern and Eastern Europe including the Grecian islands and Turkey and further east into Iran, Anatolia and the Middle East.

It is very well known that the excavations in Europe and in Palestine were seriously compromised due to destruction brought about by marauders from Eastern Europe (the Indo-Europeans) and from religious zealots in the Middle East. They wanted to be sure that the Great Mother would be only known as the Earth Mother and her religion only a fertility cult.

In fact, patriarchy has assigned this limited "fertility cult" role to the Great Mother throughout modern history.

However, new archaeological evidence and reevaluation of existing artifacts show that the Great Mother was so much more than this. She was revered as a deity who created the universe and its natural laws. She was also considered to be a prophetess, inventor and healer.

Gimbutas continues:

> It is inaccurate to call Paleolithic and Neolithic Goddess images 'fertility Goddesses' as is still done in archeological literature. The Goddesses are mainly life creators, not Venuses or beauties and most definitely not wives of male gods. They impersonate Life, Death and Regeneration. They are more than fertility and motherhood. [Gimbutas, *The Language of the Goddess*]

The Nag Hammadi library discovered in Egypt in 1945 reveals early Christian and Gnostic writings that tell an alternate story to the New Testament. As she wrote in her memoir, *Why Religion?*, scholar Elaine Pagels realized that although the sources in the New Testament often marginalize women and minimize their role, the secret gospels and other texts found in Egypt abound in feminine images, even feminine images for God.

The poem "Thunder, Complete Mind" found in the Nag Hammadi texts, dating from about 300 CE, personifies thunder as a feminine power. According to Elaine Pagels, the poem declares that the divine feminine presence, often unseen, shines everywhere, in all people whether they live in palaces or garbage dumps, embracing all that we are.

Instead of seeing the divine only in positive attributes like wisdom, holiness and power, Thunder presses us to envision divine energy with our "complete mind," even in terms of foolishness, shame and fear. The following is an excerpt from "Thunder, Complete Mind."

Why, you who hate me, do you love me, and hate those who love me?
You who deny me confess me, and you who confess me, deny me.
You who tell the truth about me, lie about me, and you who have lied
about me, tell the truth about me.
You who know me, be ignorant of me, and those who have not known
me, let them know me.
For I am knowledge and ignorance.
I am shame and boldness.
I am shameless; I am ashamed.
I am strength and I am fear.
I am the first and the last.
I am the one who is honored, and the one scorned.
I am the whore and the holy one.
I am incomprehensible silence,
And the voice of many sounds, the word in many forms;
I am the utterance of my name.
Do not cast anyone out, or turn anyone away.
I am the one who remains and the one who dissolves;
I am she who exists in all fear,
And strength in trembling.
I am she who cries out.
I am cast forth on the face of the earth.
[Barnwell and Meyer, *The Gnostic Bible*]

Many temples, shrines and artifacts dedicated to the Mother Goddess have been found in Neolithic excavations all across Europe and in the Middle East and in the early centuries of recorded history. The Great Mother was revered from the beginning of the Neolithic era, around 7,000 BCE, until the closing of the last temples dedicated to the Goddess, around 500 CE. However, the roots of the veneration to the Goddess go back to the Upper Paleolithic, 25,000 BCE, according to Marija Gambutas in *The Living Goddess*.

Deep down, many people of all genders know who they are and where they come from. According to Marija Gambutas in *The Living Goddess*:

The reconstruction of the pre-Indo-European social structure of Old Europe
is possible if various sources from different disciplines are used: linguistic, historical, mythological, religious, archaeological. Evidence from these disciplines
shows that the Paleolithic and Neolithic Old European social structure was
matrilineal, with the succession to the throne and inheritance passing through

the female line. The society was organized around a theocratic, democratic temple community guided by a highly respected priestess and her brother (or uncle); a council of women served as a governing body. In all of Old Europe, there is no evidence for the Indo-European type of patriarchal chieftainate.

The Etruscans of central Italy preserved matrifocal customs. This culture flourished from the eighth century BCE onward, but it fell into decline after the fifth century when it began a gradual assimilation into the Roman Empire. The names of Etruscan women reflected their legal and social status, in sharp contrast to Roman customs, where a woman had no name of her own. In fact, before a Roman woman was married, she was known as her father's daughter and after marriage she was known as her husband's wife. In contrast to Roman women, Etruscan women played important roles as priestesses and seers, and they were a force in politics. [Gimbutas, *The Living Goddess*]

We are connected through our unbroken ancestral line to that time in pre-recorded history when we honored the sacred feminine. She was venerated for at least 7,500 years, in comparison with the 4,000 years of patriarchal domination and the supremacy of a male god. There are at least 3,500 more years of predominance of the female divinity compared to the subsequent religions that worship the male god. How different the world would be if we had been able to follow a more feminine model of creation!

In almost all of the ancient cultures of Europe and the Middle East, the Divine Mother was not only believed to have created all the people, simultaneously in pairs, but She was also the creator of the Earth and the sky. She was revered in the same way that later the masculine god was revered, but in a different way because the inherent nature of the Goddess was that of a benevolent mother, where there wasn't guilt or shame of the body.

When I was in Barcelona in the winter of 2019 and while I was editing this book, my youngest sister, Izaskun Casado, read the manuscript and told me about the story of Lilith. Hearing about Lilith, who is believed by some scholars to be the first wife of Adam, I felt she was a missing link in my book. When a myth is conceived and understood literally, it can create and empower prejudices as divine revelation. In Lilith's story, which I recount below, we can see how Yahweh's priests have twisted the Great Mother myth of creation. Through Lilith we can perceive how deep the wound inflicted to the Sacred Feminine is. For the Great Mother, all of her creations are her beloved children. She is the embodiment of love, benevolence and wisdom. To turn the Great Mother, represented by Lilith, into a child-eating demon is a deep trauma that pervades the collective unconscious of humankind – the turning of the Sacred Masculine principle against the Sacred Feminine.

According to Genesis 1:27, the male God created male and female equally and together. This myth was adapted from an earlier legend of creation in which the Great Mother created men and women equally. The equality of men and women from Genesis 1 was later rectified with Eve. In Genesis 2:21-22, the female is created after the male and out of his body.

Lilith arose as an attempt to make sense of the difference between the two creation myths in Genesis. We can trace Lilith's origins to the Sumerian Queen of Heaven, "Lil" which meant "air" or "dust." In *The Myth of the Goddess*, Anne Baring and Jules Cashford wrote:

> …Lilith's assumption of the role of equal partner is treated in legend as insubordination, so the story goes, as she would not agree to her "proper place," which was apparently to lie beneath Adam in sexual intercourse: "Why should I lie beneath you when I am your equal since both of us were created from dust?" she asks. Adam doesn't have an answer to that one, so, uttering the magic name of God, she flies away to the wilderness of the Red Sea.
> [Baring and Cashford, *The Myth of The Goddess*]

The legend continues saying that while in exile at the Red Sea, Lilith gave birth to broods of demons to the number of more than a hundred a day. She is said to have roamed all over the world, searching for the children who deserve to be punished and killed. The Great Mother was turned into a demon that eats children!

Yahweh tries again and provides Adam with a wife who is subservient. Eve, however, is no more successful than Lilith. Eve had no independent identity since she was created out of Adam's rib and she was made to break the only commandment there was.

Lilith was not only said to kill children but also she could take possession of a man while he slept.

> If he were to find traces of semen when he awoke, he would then know that Lilith had had intercourse with him. It is hard to escape the conclusion that Lilith became an image of denied sexual desire, repressed and projected on to the female, who thereby becomes the seducer. Amulets guarding against Lilith's 'power' were found everywhere.
> [Baring and Cashford, *The Myth of the Goddess*]

When I was young girl of seven years old, I remember my aunt Titi putting amulets of *azabache*, a semiprecious stone made of carbon, on my younger siblings to protect them. At the time, of course, I didn't know where this legend came from nor did my aunt Titi. It is one of those superstitions that are passed down from time immemorial and their origins get lost.

In Genesis 3, the breaking of Yahweh's commandment is the cause of expulsion from the Garden of Eden into the human condition. The first thing Adam and Eve are said to have realized is that they were naked and they felt shame. That shame morphed into sinful sexuality. Lilith was identified with the serpent. There are numerous paintings from early Christianity to the present day that depict the serpent as a woman, supposedly Lilith. Sometimes, the serpent is portrayed as Eve. Thus Lilith was made to represent the darker side of Eve and the view that sexuality is ungodly.

Lilith's shadow erupted in the fifteenth century CE, when thousands of women were accused of being witches who copulated with demons, killed infants and seduced men. Now in the year 2020, we are going through a pandemic of COVID-19. The hospitals don't have enough capacity to tend to all the sick people with the virus. I wonder if we have awakened the dark side of the Goddess, of the planet, of nature. Many called her Kali. Interestingly enough the Coronavirus largely spares the children and the voiceless creatures. We are traversing through the dark night of the planet. How much more suffering do we have to endure before we wake up collectively?

In the many places where the Goddess was known, she was considered to be the Original Creatrix, patroness of sexual pleasures and reproduction. Through the research of professors Izak Cornelius (*The Many Faces of the Goddess*, 2004), Johanna Stuckey (*The Holy One, Qedesh[et], Lady of Heaven, Mistress of All the Gods, Eye of Ra, Without Her Equal*, 2007) and others, we know that the priestesses, considered sacred or saintly women (*qadesh* as they were known in Egypt), celebrated this aspect of the Goddess by making love in the temples. This has been documented by the scholars mentioned above from artifacts from the Late Bronze Age in 1500-1200 BCE, unearthed in Canaan located in present-day Lebanon, Syria, Jordan, and Israel. I am not saying that we should return to the practice of making love in the temples. I am pointing out the fact that in those times, body, nature and matter were not shamed yet. Today, making love in the temples would be seen by almost all cultures as something immoral, scandalous and impossible to comprehend. However, wherever the Goddess was worshipped, it was not only natural but also sacred.

The people in Canaan worshipped the priestesses because they believed the priestess was the embodiment of the Goddess. A priestess was believed to be able to see into the future by being in communion with the female deity who possessed the wisdom of the universe. Her religion, far from a fertility cult, consisted of a complex theological structure.

Evidence shows that the religion of the Goddess didn't disappear in a natural way but that it was the victim of more than 20 centuries of continual persecution from those who were promoting the new religions that worshiped the male deities as supreme. The first invasions were from the Kurgan culture in the Pontic steppe north of the Black Sea, who were most likely speakers of the Proto-Indo-European language. Different waves of Indo-European tribes from around 3000 to the 1200 BCE encroached upon the Old European cultures. Archaeologists and ethnographers working within Marija Gimbutas's Kurgan hypothesis believe that the evidence points to migrations and invasions of the peoples who spoke Indo-European languages at the beginning of the Bronze Age. According to Gimbutas's version of the Kurgan hypothesis, Old Europe was invaded and destroyed by horse-riding pastoral nomads from the Pontic-Caspian steppe (the Kurgan culture) who brought with them violence, patriarchy, and Indo-European languages.

With the arrival of the Indo-European tribes, from 3000 to 1200 BCE, masculine gods started to appear – first, as companions to the Goddess but inferior to her in status and esteem. In the Middle East with the rise of the Hebrew people and after about seven centuries of terrible massacres and persecutions, the masculine god gained total supremacy in 500 BCE.

But not all the Hebrew people were in favor of the masculine god. The priest caste of the Hebrews, who came from the tribe of Levi and were called Levites, kept the Hebrew people in line. Yahweh, through Moses, who was also a Levite, commanded the Levites to destroy those who worshiped the Golden Calf at the foot of Mount Sinai (Exodus 32:27-29) and to destroy all traces of the Goddess religion in Canaan (Numbers 33:50-52).

The biblical verse Numbers 33:50-52 states,

> Then the LORD spoke to Moses in the plains of Moab by the Jordan opposite Jericho, saying, "Speak to the sons of Israel and say to them, 'When you cross over the Jordan into the land of Canaan, then you shall drive out all the inhabitants of the land from before you, and destroy all their figured stones, and destroy all their molten images and demolish all their high places.'"

The Levites were responsible for many of the massacres which completely destroyed the religion of the Mother Goddess.

According to Yahweh's orders, all pagans were to be killed. *Pagan* was the name given to all the followers of the religion of the Goddess as well as other religions and practices out of step with the Hebrew God. The massacres were part of the continuous campaign to erase the name of the Goddess and all of her memories from the face of the Earth. In the pages of the Old Testament, Yahweh exhorts again and again, "You should slay them all, young and old, small children and women" (Ezek. 9:4-7). This section of Ezekiel claims that the people of Jerusalem were doing such utterly detestable things as honoring gods other than the Hebrew god and thus deserved to be killed.

The bloody massacres and the demolition of statues and shrines dedicated to the Goddess are recorded in the Bible as obeying the commands of Yahweh:

> You should destroy completely all the places where the nations that you have disposed of had served their gods, in the mountains, under their trees; smash

their pillars, underneath their sacred posts, burn the image of their gods and erase their name from that place. [Deut. 12:2-3]

Even though the destruction was massive, temples demolished, people of all genders and their children massively killed, and entire villages wiped from the face of the Earth, many objects survived the persecutions and continue to speak of the extent and development of the civilizations that honored the Mother Goddess. Gimbutas writes:

> The Goddess gradually retreated into the depths of forests or onto mountain tops, where she remains to this day in folk beliefs and fairy tales. Human alienation from the vital roots of earthly life ensued, the results of which are clear in our contemporary society. But the cycles never stop turning, and now we find the Goddess reemerging from the forests and mountains, bringing us hope for the future, returning us to our most ancient human roots.
> [Gimbutas, *The Language of the Goddess*]

Buddhist scholar Keith Dowman affirms that Buddhism assimilated the religion of the Mother Goddess. Dowman explains in his book, *Sky Dancer*, how the practice of Buddhism expanded over the centuries to include all sectors of Indian society. First it catered to the ascetic and the monk. Later, laypeople were included through the bodhisattva ideal. Then, as Buddhism evolved in India, the Goddess religions and practices were incorporated. Dowman writes:

> In the mature efflorescence of Indian spiritual genius Buddhism assimilated the cult of the Mother Goddess; in the Buddhist Tantra mysticism and magic, ritual and incantation, characterize the path of the yogin who does not abandon the senses and emotions but uses them as the means to attain Buddhahood during his lifetime. The Bodhisattvas acquired consorts, pairs of deities represented every conceivable mode of being, and the mystery of Buddhahood was expressed in terms of the union of sexual duality.
> [Dowman, *Sky Dancer: The Secret Life and Songs of the Lady Yeshe Tsogyel*]

These Tantric traditions of Hinduism and Buddhism appeared in India at about 500 CE. They later spread and influenced other Eastern religious traditions such as Jainism, the Tibetan Bön tradition, Taoism and the Japanese Shinto tradition. I believe that the Goddess Practices, which I present in the second part of this book, come from the time of the religion of the Mother Goddess. The Tibetan Bön tradition kept these practices safe in the Himalayas since ancient times. In the first millennium of the Common Era, Bön merged with Tibetan Buddhism and became Bön Tibetan Buddhism. The worship of dakinis originated in India prior to the eighth century and then spread into Tibet.

All of my life has been about the recovery of the Sacred Feminine in the world and in myself. The development of our patriarchal civilization that is currently destroying our planet was rooted in the suppression, persecution and denial of the Sacred Feminine. As an immediate consequence of this denial, the soul of all people split. This kind of denial has also been prevalent in Zen.

Hardly any Zen koans in the traditional Zen collections mention women. One of those rare koans is "Sei and her soul are separated" [Shibayama, *Zen Comments on the Mumonkan*, Case 38]. This koan was based on an ancient Chinese ghost story. It refers to a young woman whose soul split in two. Soul in this context can be understood as our deepest heart. One Sei is obedient to her father to whom she belongs according to the rules of patriarchy. She represents the shadow of all human beings and the planet. The other Sei, the one who goes off to live a life of freedom with her beloved, represents our awareness.

In our present situation of ecological calamity, it is imperative that we wake up our deepest heart, which has been dormant in the shadows since the beginning of recorded history. It is imperative that we use our awareness to reinstate the Sacred Feminine in union with the Sacred Masculine as co-creators of the Cosmos. This balance will bring healing to the Earth and sanity to all sentient beings.

10

The Shadow of Eve

Shishin Roshi and I have been a couple now for more than twenty years. I haven't talked very much to anyone about the beginnings of our relationship. Maybe that's because everyone assumes that they know what happened. They project onto me the same darkness that was projected on Eve and Lilith, the temptresses, the sinners and the whores, in the Garden of Eden. People thought that if Shishin Roshi did not take advantage of me sexually, abusing his power, then for sure I must have seduced him like the snake tempted Adam in the Garden of Eden. I have been slandered many times and I have also felt the envy of women, because I was the "chosen one." I think that being a Hispanic woman, rather than an Anglo woman, added another element to the negative responses I received. I always felt a lot of empathy for the Sixth Ancestor of our tradition, Huineng. Although he was an illiterate and humble layman, he was very enlightened. The Fifth Ancestor recognized him as his successor on their first encounter when he asked Huineng,

> "Where do you come from?"
> "I come from the South," responded Huineng.
> "Men from the South do not have Buddha Nature," responded the Fifth Ancestor.
> Huineng replied, "Although there is South and North in the minds of men, there is no South or North in Buddha Nature."
> [Price and Mou-Lam, *The Diamond Sutra and the Sutra of Hui Neng*]

The Fifth Ancestor recognized that Huineng was well-grounded in his Buddha Nature and felt he had to protect his future successor from the envy of the other monks. He was afraid someone would murder Huineng since he was an illiterate layman whom the monks would not be willing to accept as an heir to the dharma.

I met Shishin about six months after I left Pat Hawk Roshi. I was very fed up with Zen and did not know if I could go back to it. I became a member of Shishin's center, Great

Mountain Zen Center, in order to have a private interview with him.

During my first interview with Shishin Sensei, I felt he was assuming that his training was superior to mine. I did not like that assumption. I told him that I had already gone through a lot and that I was not going to take any more of that kind of treatment. I left the interview room with a decision not to come back.

About a month later I received a call from him. I was so surprised that he had even noticed my absence and he even asked me to come back and sit in zazen with them. I accepted. This second time was much better, and I did not feel any superiority attitude. I resumed koan practice with him, but first he had to test me in some very important koans. He needed to be sure that I was where I said I was.

As Shishin writes in his memoir *My American Zen Life*:

> When Shinko came to practice with me, she was full of fire in a way that reminded me of myself about twenty years earlier. She constantly probed and questioned. In dokusan, I tested her understanding of the Buddha Dharma as best I could to make sure that she was not all bluster. Every Zen barrier I erected, she was able to pass through. [Wick, *My American Zen Life*]

After he tested me to his satisfaction, I was able to tell him about the Lady of Light. After returning from visiting Tsultrim Allione and with the knowledge that I was having dakini experiences, I was able to resume my koan practice with him. I was already in the last book of koans and he treated me with respect.

I had never been interested physically in any of my teachers. I was practicing to clarify my mind and I did not care about the teachers as much as I cared about the teachings. The teachers were for me only the temporary vehicle that the teachings flowed from.

Yet I started growing fond of Shishin. My encounters with him in dokusan were always in a heightened and luminous state of mind. From the depths of this luminosity, deep love arose in both of us. It was as if the Earth had opened up and from her belly this ancient love showed up. He treasured my insight and for the first time in my life I felt the presence of a very kind and non-judgmental being. What do you do when something of this magnitude happens? Do you renounce it? We did try to renounce it, but it was much bigger than us. We stopped seeing each other. He was married and I was separated but not divorced.

Shishin decided to cut the relationship with me completely. I thought I was going to die of pain, but I understood that trying to save his marriage was most important. I stopped sitting with his group. After a few weeks of no communication, Shishin contacted me to say that he had tried but that he couldn't fix his marriage and that he was separating too. I started sitting with his group again. His wife found our love emails from before. Hell broke loose. Shishin and I had the choice to go separate ways. For sure, this would have satisfied the sangha and ended our troubles, but we couldn't betray this love that had arisen from a deep place beyond our understanding. We decided to stick together against all odds.

Some members of Great Mountain Zen Center harassed me. I received nasty calls and emails. I was afraid that some of them might hurt me or hurt my kids. I felt like a cornered animal trying to protect her young. I asked a lawyer friend of mine to send a letter to those who were harassing me, threatening to take them to court. The harassment stopped and I felt my kids were safe.

It just so happened that Bernie Glassman Roshi, the senior teacher in our lineage, was in Boulder leading a workshop and heard about our troubles. He came to our house and heard our story. What I wrote before was wrong. I said nobody asked me what had happened, but I wasn't correct. Bernie Glassman did ask me what had happened. I felt that he believed us, and I did not feel any judgments coming from him. Since Shishin was a teacher and in a position of power and I was a student, our relationship could be viewed as an abuse of power. But it wasn't. It was a deep love that continues today. Bernie understood and he said that we needed to perform a healing council with the sangha. He also said that because I was Puerto Rican, he should send his sangha members Paco and his wife Noemi to lead the council because they were also Puerto Rican. We felt open to the idea of healing our sangha. Some sangha members came to the council, others didn't. Most people were angry, but at the third round to the council circle we felt that healing was taking place. Some people left the sangha, others stayed with us till this day.

Shishin and I each got divorced. We found a propitious house in Lafayette to house our Zen Center. It overlooked a park, Waneka Lake. It was nice because people could leave their cars at the lake and walk through the park to get to the back of the house. We were happy that we had found this house where we could start a residential Zen training. Eventually Shishin named me his successor and we started teaching together.

After ten years of teaching, I began to lose my enthusiasm. It was revived by meeting Roshi Wendy Egyoku Nakao, Abbot of the Zen Center of Los Angeles (ZCLA). I first met her at several White Plum Asanga meetings. The White Plum Asanga is the formal name of our lineage. Then I got to know her better when she helped perform our wedding ceremony. I connected more deeply with her when I raised my voice trying to stop the repeated sexual abuse of power by a male teacher in the White Plum. We had a council for White Plum teachers that Roshi Egyoku generously led at ZCLA. The nature of the council was confidential so I cannot spell what went on there, but I can say that it was a very healing council and women's voices were heard.

After teaching together with Shishin Roshi for more than twelve years, I could have received *Inka*, empowerment as a Zen Roshi, from him. Actually he'd been ready to give me Inka for a while, but I couldn't accept it. Although it had been a blessing to teach Zen together, it had also been a source of suffering for me. The few times that I tried to include my personal story as part of my Dharma talks, even a year after teaching with Shishin in Lafayette, I was heavily attacked by some of the men in the sangha. To accept the formal Inka empowerment from my partner would undercut my authority.

Shishin talked to Roshi Egyoku and explained the situation to her. She was willing to give me Inka transmission but first she wanted to get to know me more intimately prior to an empowerment ceremony. I participated in several retreats at ZCLA over the following year and I gave several talks. The first talk I gave was called, guess what? The Garden of Eden! The talk was very well-received, and I felt loved at ZCLA. I also fell in love with the ZCLA sangha and Roshi Egyoku. I felt that even if I had been half woman and half horse, they would have accepted me. The year that I spent in close connection with Roshi Egyoku was one of the most joyful years of my life. I spent time in her house when in LA and went back and forth to Colorado. One night, when we finished a very lively discussion, which I cannot disclose here since it was confidential, she took out some cups from a top shelf in her kitchen cabinet and poured some tea in them. She took the cups to her living room and said something like, "These are the Guan Yin cups and they represent transmission." I had tears flowing down my cheeks in deep gratitude to her compassionate heart. I had no words to express my deep feelings.

11

The Priestess and the Snake

*I*n the year 2015, I formally received Inka transmission from Roshi Wendy Egyoku Nakao, abbot of the Zen Center of Los Angeles, and I could call myself a Zen Roshi or Zen Master. After so many years of searching, I finally found a woman of wisdom in my own tradition and my own lineage! Roshi Egyoku understood my experiences and encouraged me to spread the Wisdom Seed of the Great Mother.

Roshi Egyoku wrote the following verse on my empowerment rakusu, the vestment a Zen Buddhist wears as a mark of his or her commitment to follow the Way of the Buddha. The name Ekai means Ocean of Wisdom. It was the name given to me in 2004 during my empowerment ceremony by Shishin Roshi when I became a Sensei, or independent teacher.

> Ekai Shinko, life after life, birth after birth,
> May the Body of Light illumine the Great Ocean.
> Never falter!
> Do not let die the wisdom seed of the Great Mother of the Buddhas!
> Truly, I implore you.

As a Zen Roshi, I hold dokusan, private interviews, with those who practice meditation and want direction in their practice, or who want to hear my suggestions regarding some problem they might be having in their lives. Sometimes they just want me to listen to them.

In Mesopotamia, the priestesses were considered sacred, holy women who were able to see into the future. Mesopotamia, the crib of civilization, was the old name of the regions located between the Tigris and Euphrates rivers which cover present-day Iraq, Jordan, Syria, Lebanon, Kuwait and parts of Iran. From Greece to Mesopotamia, the remains of numerous temples and oracular shrines from the Neolithic era have been found in which the priestesses of the Mother Goddess gave military, political and personal counsel to those who came looking for it. For the priestesses, the future was not something determined by uncontrollable fates but was something malleable, something that we could act upon if we would know the most beneficial actions to take.

Psychic abilities are something that can happen as part of developing a deep meditation practice. However, this is not something that we pursue. It is more like a side effect. Since at a deep level we are all connected and time doesn't exist in the absolute sense, it is not surprising that sometimes we can see fragments of the future.

On September 7, 2001, before I received Inka from Roshi Egyoku, I had an important dream when I was at Great Mountain Zen Center with Shishin Roshi. I was inside a building in flames. I saw other buildings collapsing. Time stopped inside the dream. I had a message that I had to gather the people and start prayer circles. I did that in the dream. I gathered the people who were around the city and we started prayer circles. It was a disturbing dream. It was so real. In the morning I couldn't stop thinking about it. I painted it over and over. I showed my paintings to Shishin Roshi and I said to him, "It surely looks like New York City."

He was going on a trip to Utah for a week and he left me in charge of the Zen Center. Then a few days later the terrorist attack happened at the World Trade Center, the Twin Towers, in New York City. That same day, I started the prayer circles at the Great Mountain Zen Center, and this is the prayer that arose. We call it the Prayer for Peace.

> All Buddhas, Bodhisattvas,
> Protectors of the Dharma,
> And the Three Treasures,
> With all sentient beings
> I open my heart to transform,
> Ignorance, violence and suffering,
> May healing and Peace prevail
> Throughout the Dharma Worlds.
> Maha, Prajna, Paramita

Nineteen years later, we continue reciting this prayer as part of our chanting services during retreats.

It seems clear to me now that the origin of the Catholic practice of confession was a deviation from the priestesses' tradition of giving advice to the people. In Christianity, the body and the flesh and even our human nature are seen as sources of evil. [*See* Galatians 5:19-21 and Romans 7:5 as examples.]

On the contrary, Zen Buddhism can bring us to experience that our nature is a source of pure goodness. This is in part why I love Zen Buddhism so much. However, this nature is obscured due to our deluded thoughts. Through meditation we can see beyond the veil of thoughts into our own true nature of goodness. To do this takes practice and determination, but anyone can realize it.

I remember when I was seven years old, I was obliged to take the first communion and to go to confession. I was taught that if you do not confess all of your sins, you commit a venial or mortal sin, depending on the degree of the unconfessed sin. I did not want to confess to the priest how much I liked to have my body pressed against a boy I liked. Ever since the episode with my aunt Titi, I thought that pressing my body against a boy must be considered a mortal sin for sure and undoubtedly the punishment must be hell.

I remember standing in front of the confessionary waiting in line for my first confession: the heat of the tropics, the fans turning above my head making a squeaking sound, the *coquís* singing outside – tiny frogs indigenous to Puerto Rico – and me sweating the sweats of hell inside the church. Those were hours of tremendous suffering for me. When it was finally my turn to enter the confessionary, I did not tell the priest what I had done, therefore committing another mortal sin. As if that were not enough, then I went to receive the communion so that my aunt would think that I had confessed all of my sins. In my mind, that implied another mortal sin. Oh my! I always felt I was in such trouble!

One day, however, I did tell the priest "Yo hice fresquerías con un niño." I had been fresh with a boy. I felt so scared when the priest seemed to show a lot of interest in it and started to ask me all kinds of questions like, "What exactly did you do? Where did you do it? How old was the boy?" He dismissed me with the usual Hail Mary and Our Father after he extracted the information he sought. After that day I thought that I would rather die in mortal sin and go to hell than have another conversation like that with a man behind a veil whose face I couldn't see. Of course it would not have been any better to see his face.

Since I thought I was accumulating so many mortal sins, the evenings were particularly scary to me. In Puerto Rico, we lived in a house with huge wooden doors that opened up to our back yard. The sunset views were panoramic from inside the house when the wooden doors were opened, which they always were except at night or when there was bad weather. The intense and dramatic reds, oranges and yellows of sunset reminded me of hell. Almost every evening, unless it was cloudy or rainy, I felt such an intense fear that sometimes I had to go and hide under my bed. On these occasions I did not see the Lady of Light.

Writing these pages, I realize now that even if I felt intense fear, I did not stay present with the fear like I did when I was five-and-a-half years old. I protected myself from the fear by hiding under my bed; therefore, I did not enter into the Sambhogakaya realm. What a pity! It is not the same to feel one's emotions thoroughly as it is to feel them halfway and then defend against them. How to feel emotions thoroughly so that they can transform into enlightened wisdom is the topic of the book I wrote with Shishin Roshi, *The Great Heart Way*. We also developed a series of Great Heart workshops, which we continue to offer regularly.

The intense fear and suffering I felt did not stop me from continuing to do *fresquerías* with the boys. That was heaven to me. It reminds me of the verse that the famous Zen Master Ikkyu (1394-1481) wrote. Ikkyu's eccentric behavior was not typical, yet he was accepted as enlightened. His behavior demonstrated for later generations that in Zen there are no absolute prohibitions against sexuality, etc.

> With a young beauty, I am engrossed in fervent love-play;
> We sit in a pavilion, a pleasure girl and this Zen monk.
> I am enraptured by hugs and kisses
> And certainly do not feel as if I am burning in hell.
> [Stevens, *Three Zen Masters: Ikkyu, Hakuin, Ryokan*]

In the religion of the Goddess, the snake was a very important symbol. In the oldest myths, from Paleolithic Greece and Mesopotamia, creation started with a serpent, which was known as "The Divine Lady Serpent" or the "Great Mother Serpent of the Sky" and was a symbol of clairvoyance and mystical wisdom. The priestesses were believed to be in communion with the Divine Lady Serpent of the Sky.

From ancient times until the mid-twentieth century in the Baltic region, which includes Lithuania, Latvia, Finland and Estonia, harmless green snakes often shared the house with people. They occupied a place of honor, the sacred corner of the house, and were fed milk in addition to their regular diet. The snake protected the family, or more exactly, symbolized its life force. It was believed that whoever killed the snake would destroy the happiness of the whole family and would be paralyzed for the rest of his or her life. The serpent's vital influence extended not only to fertility and growth, but to the regeneration of dying life-energy. Through the sloughing of the old skin and regeneration of the new skin, the snake possessed potent powers in healing and creating life.

Through the Neolithic era, portrayals of the Snake Goddess consistently featured a crown-like headpiece. This image lives on in Baltic and other European folklore in the belief that some snakes are crowned, and these crowns are symbols of wisdom and wealth. The crown enables one to know all, to see hidden treasures, and to understand the language of animals. According to Gimbutas, these myths and fairy tales about the sacredness of snakes hark back to the Neolithic snake Goddess. [Gimbutas, *The Living Goddess*]

In Egypt, the cobra with a raised hood represented the Great Mother. We later see this symbol on the forehead of Egyptian royalty. In the moments before his ultimate enlightenment, a legend says, a great cobra protected the Buddha. The cobra opened up its hood like a huge umbrella over his whole body to protect him from balls of fire sent by Mara, the archetype of delusion and the embodiment of temptation. Since the cobra was a symbol of the Great Mother, this legend could be another indication that Buddhism had assimilated the religion of the Great Mother. Of course, in the patriarchal Judeo-Christian era, the serpent symbol was turned into a symbol of evil, which, abetted by the woman, caused humans to be cast out of Eden.

Perhaps the most powerful weapon used in the campaign to suppress the religion of the female deity could be the story of Adam and Eve. The origin of the Genesis myth of Adam and Eve is not clear; nor is it clear whether there were other versions under consideration when Genesis was written. There is some evidence from British scholars Anne Baring and Jules Cashford (*The Myth of the Goddess; Evolution of an Image*) that the Adam and Eve myth originated from Sumerians who lived in what is now modern Iraq. They claim that "The Old and New Testaments are saturated with images that came originally from Sumeria." The idea for Adam's birth-giving rib came from a Sumerian childbirth-Goddess, Nin-ti, known as Lady of the Rib. Baring and Cashford write: "Since ti means both 'rib' and 'life,' she was also Lady of Life. She made infants' bones in utero from their mothers' ribs, which is why biblical writers thought ribs possessed the magic of maternity."

It was very important for the patriarchs to achieve religious supremacy and power by demeaning, demonizing and suppressing the wisdom of women. Therefore, it was crucial that in the Garden of Eden myth, Adam and Eve didn't decide to eat the forbidden fruit together, but that the woman ate first upon the advice of the serpent.

The serpent here symbolizes the Great Mother and specifically, Lilith. In the Genesis story, the snake was the symbol of the Great Mother and as such the serpent was made to seduce and tempt the original couple. It is my insight that Eve was used to impersonate the priestess of the Great Mother tradition, who by listening to the Goddess was said to cause the fall of humankind. As a result, many centuries of oracular divination and the inherent wisdom and morality of women were discredited. With the creation of this myth, we have been deprived of the imagery of a true and benevolent Mother Goddess, who embodied the creative powers of the universe itself. For wasn't it the woman Eve who, by listening to the advice of a serpent, eating the forbidden fruit, and suggesting that man try it too, had caused the downfall and misery of all humankind?

In this fable, sexual drive was not to be regarded as the natural biological process that encourages the human species to reproduce itself, but it was to be viewed as women's fault. The snake was made into a source of evil and anyone who adhered to the prophetesses of the feminine religion was condemned to death.

Eve was to be severely punished, together with all women, for her offense, as the male deity decreed in Genesis 3:16,

> I will greatly multiply your pain in childbearing, in pain you shall bring forth children, yet your desire shall be for your husband and he shall rule over you.

According to the male deity, women's pain for bearing a child was to be regarded as punishment, so that all women giving birth would thus be forced to identify with Eve, the sinner.

It was of capital importance, in order to achieve the supremacy of the masculine God, that man had to be created first. So, from a very small part of man – his rib – the woman was created. Even with all the knowledge about the facts of biological birth, humanity was assured that by divine decree, men don't come from women, but women from men. How could anyone believe something like that?

From that time on, and as a result of Eve's faults and in eternal payment for it, her husband was awarded the divine right to dominate her and she was expected to submit obediently. When these decrees were proclaimed, the couple was expelled from the Garden of Eden, the original paradise where life had been so easy. From that time on, they were to labor for their livelihood. Women became property of men. By denying women their sexual freedom, men also assured themselves of their right to rule and to the throne.

Now I understand why Mary was crushing the head of a black snake in the statue I saw when I joined the nun school in Madrid when I was ten or eleven years old. Now I understand that Mary needed to be used by the church authorities as a male creation of the perfect woman, the opposite of Eve. Mary is the one who crushes the head of the snake, which symbolizes that sex and the Great Mother tradition were evil and needed to be killed. Mary was made into a new model of purity that was not real.

It makes sense to me and is my insight that Mary was a priestess in the Great Mother tradition. Making love with Joseph was for her a sacred thing. Mary had the gift of vision, like many priestesses did. She saw the angel who transmitted to her that she was pregnant and that she must flee with Joseph to protect the life of their child. If the followers of the male God found out that Mary was pregnant outside the marriage, she might have been stoned to death. According to Luke 2:5, Mary was pregnant before she and Joseph were married. It makes sense to me that the part about the immaculate conception would have been added later in the New Testament, because certainly the man known as the son of God would not have been able to be born from a woman outside of marriage. Priestesses and pregnant women outside of marriage were called whores, so it would not have sounded very good to them to say that the son of God was born from a whore!

The following poem, *sometimes I wonder*, by Kaitlin Hardy Shetler, catches the essence of what I am saying:

> sometimes I wonder
> if Mary breastfed Jesus…
> and sometimes I wonder
> if this is all too vulgar
> to ask in a church
> full of men
> without milk stains on their shirts
> or coconut oil on their breasts

preaching from pulpits off limits to The Mother of God.
but then I think of feeding Jesus,
birthing Jesus,
the expulsion of blood
and smell of sweat,
the salt of a mother's tears
onto the soft head of the salt of the Earth,
feeling lonely
and tired…
and I think,
if the vulgarity of birth is not
honestly preached
by men who carry power but not burden,
who carry privilege but not labor,
who carry authority but not submission,
then it should not be preached at all.
because the real scandal of the Birth of God
lies in the cracked nipples of a
14 year old
and not in the sermons of ministers
who say women
are too delicate
to lead.

Slowly over the years I have retreated into Maitreya Abbey where, with the help of many sangha members and Shishin, I have created a Garden of Eden, where people can come and feel love. In the year 2012, Shishin and I were married by Roshi Bernie Glassman, a few days after Bernie had installed me as the Abbess of Maitreya Abbey. Now that Bernie has passed away, I can see clearly how precious those days were.

We called our marriage ceremony "The Return to the Garden of Eden." We were married under an old apple tree in the backyard of the Abbey. Bernie performed the wedding. I had created a 20-foot snake made out of fabric and filled in with balloons to give her volume. The snake was wrapped many times around the apple tree, her head rising to the skies. We placed two swings on each side of the apple tree. Before the ceremony started, there was a chanting service. Bernie was sitting with Shishin on one of the swings and I was sitting on the other with Roshi Egyoku. During the ceremony Roshi Egyoku blew a trumpet several times. Bernie took a red apple from the tree. Shishin and I intertwined our arms together and took bites from the apple. That act completed the marriage.

Near the end of the ceremony Bernie piled the hands of the four of us together, wrapping them with a *mala*, Buddhist prayer beads, and made a sound of a rocket lifting to the skies. At the end of the ceremony, I thanked everyone for witnessing the ceremony and explained that Maitreya Abbey means The House of the Mother. When I said these words, a symphony of crickets and cicadas delighted us with the most beautiful melody. The snake was happy!

12

The Effects of the Patriarchy

*I*n the Goddess Religions, women were not the property of men and were free to take more than one lover. However, establishing paternity is one of the cornerstones of all patriarchal cultures, which insisted on controlling women's reproductive behavior. Gimbutas points out that the inability to establish paternity has an effect on social structure because, when the biological father cannot be determined, the mother and her kin are automatically the focus of the family and the family structure is matrilineal. [Gimbutas, *The Living Goddess*]

It became clear to the Levite priests that, in order to achieve religious supremacy and power, they had to have unquestionable knowledge of paternity. Deuteronomy 22:28-29 shows paternity is so important that even violent rape was equated with marriage. In Levite law, the rape of a virgin was honored as a declaration of ownership and brought about a forced marriage.

Under this new law, men were encouraged to be predators of women. Even to this day, we can see how deeply ingrained this predatory behavior toward women is in the stories we hear from the #MeToo movement.

As a result of the institution of a patriarchal system, Judaism and then Christianity developed as religions that regarded sex for pleasure as something dirty, shameful and sinful.

There are many examples in the Bible where women are denigrated for the pleasure of men. In "By Identifying Abuse in the Bible We Can Call Out injustice in Life," which appeared in the *Houston Chronicle* in 2019, Reverend Laura Mayo writes:

> Read the rape of Dinah in Genesis 34:1-31. Read the rape of the concubine in Judges 19:1-20:11. Read about the destruction of Sodom and Gomorrah in Genesis 19 – and be prepared to discover that Lot was willing to send out his own daughters to be raped by a marauding crowd. Read the book of Esther again. Esther was sex-trafficked and raped.

The story of David and Bathsheba in Samuel Chapters 11 and 12 is also open to interpretation. The prevailing version from the patriarchal perspective has Bathsheba luring David. But David was king, and what maiden could stand up to such a powerful man without dire consequences? Richard Davidson points out in "Did King David Rape Bathsheba? A Case Study in Narrative Theology" that this is a story about a "power rape, in which a person in a position of authority abuses that 'power' to victimize a subservient and vulnerable person sexually, whether or not the victim appears to give 'consent.' David, the king, appointed by God to defend the helpless and vulnerable, becomes a victimizer of the vulnerable."

In the myth of Adam and Eve, women and men alike are told that at Yahweh's divine decree, male ownership and control of submissively obedient women was to be regarded as the natural state of the human species. This was the beginning of male domination that is still prevalent to this day in most of the world.

Even in modern history, women have been persecuted en masse, including in the witch hunts of the fifteenth to eighteenth centuries.

"The murder of women accused as witches escalated to more than eight million. The burned or hanged victims were mostly simple country women who learned the lore and the secrets of the Goddess from their mothers or grandmothers," writes Marija Gimbutas in *The Language of the Goddess*.

Until about 1880, women could be punished in Western Europe and in the United States for denying men their conjugal rights. Rape within marriage was not considered rape. It took until the 1980s for the US to decree that marital rape was a crime, although not until 1993 did all 50 states protect women from marital rape, when the final two states (Oklahoma and North Carolina) got on board with the notion. Even now in 2020 in the United States of America there is a senate consisting mainly of white men who are attempting to pass laws that restrict what women can and cannot do with their own bodies.

Merlin Stone observes in *When God was a Woman*:

> The Hebrew Prophets and priests, the Levites, wrote with open and scornful contempt of any woman who was neither virgin nor married. They insisted that all woman must be publicly designated as the private property of some man, father or husband.

Does this story seem familiar to you? Many of the codes of morality that the patriarchal religions still use are derived from these laws and customs.

When I was growing up during the late 1960s and early 1970s, there were several girls I knew who got pregnant when they were still in their teens. Their families threw them out into the street. It is amazing that the Catholic Christian families of these girls still believed in such false and dishonest decrees about morality. The judgment against women's sexuality is further compounded by hypocrisy, with one rule for women and another for men. Stone continues:

Though the Bible repeatedly announced that a woman who dared to make love to a man other than her husband was a shameful and profane degradation to the entire faith, Hebrew men went about honorably collecting as many women as they could economically afford. The records of the Hebrew kings reveal that they kept large harems and most Hebrew men appear to have taken several wives; yet each of these women was expected to be totally faithful to the fragment of the husband to whom she was assigned.

The effects of the denigration and disempowerment of women have had monstrous consequences. Women were property of men. When they married, they had to vow to obey and serve their husband. Women didn't own their bodies. Since the Catholic Church saw them as an impediment for the priests to unite with God, priests were not allowed to marry.

Later, that dishonesty and falsehood became apparent when it was revealed that disheartening numbers of priests in the Catholic Church, in the absence of women or male adult partners, have been raping, during decades if not centuries, the children of the families who believed in them and in their male god. And church authorities have been covering this up for equally as long.

I don't mean to single out the Catholic Church. Similar abuse of women has prevailed in other patriarchal religions, including all branches of Christianity, Judaism and Islam. Buddhism has been predominantly patriarchal and has deprecated the role of women. That trend has been reversed in the United States and Western Europe over the past 50 years, especially in Zen Buddhism, where women have been recognized and empowered as spiritual leaders. The mystical branches of all the major religions tend to recognize the spiritual equality of men and women and are now coming to include all genders. It is the social, political and institutional levels of these patriarchal religions that inflict the most damage.

How did I personally feel the effects of patriarchy? When I ask myself that question, I feel my body tensing up and shrinking. Growing up in Spain during the dictatorship of Francisco Franco, asking myself this question would have had no meaning. I did not know anything else outside of patriarchy. I did not even have the idea that anything else was possible. I felt I had been taken from Puerto Rico into a dark world where the armed policemen, called the Grises due to their grey uniforms, could come charging inside the university campus with their clubs, their machine guns and their armor. They truly looked like Darth Vader's army but in grey, which made them even scarier. Sometimes the Grises entered the campuses of the universities in full gear and riding horses so that they could catch and hit students faster. We had no rights as students. We could be killed and disappear from this Earth and the government was not accountable. I heard of so many students who were beaten in jail until they were killed.

When I was a younger student at Las Reverandas Madres Irlandesas, all girls were educated to be married. We were not taught to think and question – questioning was actually forbidden. I hated it. But now, writing these pages, I only feel sad and tender – very tender and loving to the rebellious girl that I was. I want to hug her and tell her that it was going to be okay, that eventually we would be able to get out of that dark cloud into the vast open skies.

Being a bit mischievous at middle school is what kept me from being depressed; it gave me a bit of the electric excitement I felt riding my horse. I felt alive again when I got my revenge. For example, I would sit in the first row of chairs in class. The nun would sit on an elevated platform. Before anyone arrived, I would put one leg of her table outside the platform. The nun would come into the class to call on us individually to hear the line-by-line memorized lesson, but the moment she put her elbows on the table and leaned on it, the table would fall on top of my friend and me. Then we would steadfastly pick up the table and make the nun believe that we were good. If we had been caught doing this, we would have probably been expelled from the school. Behaving like that kept me alive; it reminded me of my paradise. Even "sinning" was good because it connected me with my true essence and the Lady of Light. However, I did not develop my own voice until I came to Zen in my thirties. Until then, I was locked in silence inside myself.

When women were denigrated and disempowered within the patriarchal religions, Mother Nature and Mother Earth were also seen as objects to dominate, rape and disrespect. Today patriarchy still rules the great majority of our world and all major religions. As a consequence, the domination, rape and exploitation of nature, the Earth and women continues unabated.

I was educated to be a good wife and to be submissive to my husband, but I never was. I went through two turbulent marriages and divorces before marrying Shishin. But I had the most beautiful kids, my two boys, whom I raised mostly as a single mother. They have been the most important beings in my life. I had started an export/import business with my second husband and the business did very well, which allowed me to study Zen and to participate in all the retreats. I was also able to hire an excellent German nanny who took care of my boys when I went to retreats. Zen retreats allowed me to unfold the Sacred Feminine inside myself, to be one with Her and to write this book.

Within my own Zen tradition, and in an effort to stop sexual abuse by male Zen teachers, I have to recognize the tireless efforts of my lineage, the White Plum Asanga. Codes of Conduct for Zen teachers and protocols for dealing with complaints were implemented when Shishin Roshi was president of White Plum. Women in the lineage have refined the guidelines and have actively dealt with teacher transgressions. I especially want to acknowledge the work of the abbot of Zen Center of Los Angeles, Roshi Wendy Egyoku Nakao, and the current president of the organization, Roshi Anne Seisen Sanders, as well as Roshi Joan Hogetsu Hoeberichts, Roshi Susan Myoyu Andersen and Roshi Jan Chozen Bays. I feel very honored to belong to this association of Zen teachers that so courageously and compassionately stands up to such abuse and provides the abuser and the abused with paths to heal. The founder of the White Plum lineage, Taizan Maezumi Roshi, was acknowledged as an important and gifted Zen Master. Nevertheless, he abused alcohol and had sexual relations with some of his female students. Through intervention by senior students, Maezumi Roshi attended a substance abuse recovery clinic. For the rest of his life, he expressed remorse for his actions and continually apologized to his community.

Even while we are reeling from shock due to the abuse and rape of children, we cannot forget what has been done for centuries to people of all genders in the name of the male god. In the name of the male god, we women were killed, raped, captured, enslaved, our children killed, raped or taken from us, our identities stolen and our bodies sold. All of these abuses are stored in our DNA. It is time to wake up from that oppressive dream to the sacred nature of who we really are! Wake up from the dream that is dictated by what others say, what the media says, what the Christian church says, and what the government wants us to believe. The truth is inside of us. The gateway to freedom is inside of us. We can wake up individually and collectively. This is also in our DNA.

13

A Body of Light

In his public speeches, the Dalai Lama has mentioned the time when the Female Deity was venerated. He referred to scientific studies that conclude that women respond more strongly than men to suffering and that women are much more empathetic than men. "Biologically women are more sensitive," he said. And he added that since women usually take the major role in raising children, the compassion, happiness and satisfaction of future generations depends on mothers. Citing scientific studies, the Dalai Lama considers women to be the biological nexus for spreading warm-heartedness. He believes that there would be less violence if women played a more active role in society.

During the 2009 Vancouver Peace Conference, the Dalai Lama said that the World will be saved by the Western Women. When reading an early version of this manuscript, my friend, writer, editor and Sensei in our lineage, Sean Tetsudo Murphy noted, "It is time for the feminine to step forward, for patriarchy certainly has not worked!"

In *Women of Wisdom*, Tsultrim Allione writes:

> According to Namkhai Norbu Rinpoche, Garab Dorje,... the founder of the Dzog Chen teachings, went so far as to say that the majority of those who could reach the ultimate level of the Dzog Chen teachings, the manifestation of the body of light, or the rainbow body, would be women. The rainbow body manifests at the time of death. The physical body completely disappears except for the hair and the fingernails, and a body of light is formed from the essence of the elements. This body can be perceived by those in very open states of mind. Namkhai Norbu Rinpoche explains that the reason for the predominance of women achieving the rainbow body is that women had a natural affinity in working with energy and vision and the Dzog Chen practices leading toward the body of light are connected to working directly with energy and vision, rather than logic and intellectual studies.
> [Allione, *Women of Wisdom*]

When I read this for the first time I thought, "I knew it! I knew it! This is what I want! This is what I want!" When I joined the sangha of Shishin Roshi, I asked him if I could take the lay precepts, the Buddhist code of ethics, again. I had taken them before when I was studying with Roshi Philip Kapleau. The reason for wanting to take the precepts again was in order to receive a new dharma name that would motivate me further in my practice. My name until then was Fire Lotus. That name had served me for many years, but I did not connect with it any longer. Now my practice and my spiritual understanding had matured, and I longed for the name Body of Light. Shishin Roshi needed to find the *kanji* ideograms in Japanese before he could tell me how this name would sound. I waited patiently for more than a month. Then finally one day he said, "It's Shinko!"

Shinko? Hm! I liked it! Since that day, more than 15 years ago, I have been Shinko.

Realizing the body of light in life and at the time of death is the motivational energy behind my spiritual practice. Like Garab Dorje, I believe that many women have a natural way to understand energy and vision and therefore we could manifest the body of light in life as in death. I truly believe that the Goddess Practices I present in the second part of this book are a vehicle to manifest our body of light.

In the year 2007, we were holding a Great Heart Retreat at our Zen Center which at the time was in Lafayette, Colorado. We had invited a facilitator to help us teach the part about Voice Dialogue. We use this technique in groups when everyone is not a strong practitioner of zazen. The Voice Dialogue techniques help to quiet the loud mental voices so that the person, once the inner voices are quiet, can start venturing on her own to feel the body directly.

While the Voice Dialogue teacher was instructing the group, I started to have visions of a horse and a house in the country. The visions were so clear. I drew the house in the country, and I drew the horse. They seemed so real.

After the retreat I went and found the horse of my visions. I found an ad for a horse on Craigslist and immediately went to see her in south Denver. She belonged to a family that was having financial troubles. I was happy to help them out and to adopt the horse. She was the first horse I saw and I quickly bonded with her. I found some stables near the Zen Center. The rent was very reasonable and I was able to board her there.

Oh, a horse! I had never dreamed I could own a horse again. When I smelled her, her smell connected me with my childhood, my freedom, my wildness. It also connected me with my beautiful island, the palm trees I adore, the coconut water, the dirt, the grass, the soil, my roots.

I called my new mare Naga. *Nagas* are serpentine creatures that were said to have kept the Buddhist scriptures safe for some time until people were ready to receive them. According to the legend of Nagarjuna, the Fourteenth Ancestor of Indian Buddhism, he traveled deep into the Earth through his meditative powers to the lair of the Naga King, who had been entrusted by the Buddha with the *Prajna Paramita Sutra*. Seeing that Nagarjuna was the one prophesied by Shakyamuni Buddha, the Naga King gave these texts to him to bring back to the surface.

It so happened that one day the owner of the stables where Naga was being boarded had left some barbwire around the fields and Naga had injured her legs. I asked the owner of the stables to remove the barbwire, but he said he wouldn't. I decided I had to find a better home for my horse.

At about the same time, in the year 2008, a little house I owned close to the Zen Center sold. I talked with the real estate agent who sold it and asked him to find a horse property within 30 miles of Lafayette. The next day, after the sale of the house was completed, the real estate agent brought us to the place where I live now, Maitreya Abbey. This place was in great need of repairs. Once we had made it habitable, I moved there with Naga.

Shishin Roshi came to visit the Abbey very often. Then two residents who were living at the Zen Center in Lafayette decided they wanted to help us clean up the property and do some remodeling of the buildings. Then the whole Zen Center sangha wanted to help. The roofs were falling down on parts of the buildings. Many members of the Zen Center came and together we ripped off the old roof. Great Mountain Zen Center raised money to hire a company to install a new roof.

Now Maitreya Abbey is the home of Great Mountain Zen Center. It has become a very beautiful property. We remodeled all the buildings and did a lot of the work ourselves. We rescued several animals including two goats, two horses, one rooster, one dog, one cat and seven hens, creating a small animal sanctuary. During retreats, taking care of the animals is part of the samu or work practice. We have built our first green house and we are growing vegetables through the winter that provide food for ourselves and the residents. We use well water for irrigation. We take all of our leaves and branches from our many trees to a compost center twenty miles away. We have compost bins for food scraps and we take our recycling to a recycling center a few miles away. At the moment, we have four residents in our community who help take care of the property and the programs. The most remarkable feature we offer to our community is a relationship based on *The Great Heart Way*. We talk openly and honestly about how we feel and we use the model of Native American Council to resolve conflicts when they emerge. In the year 2012 Bernie Glassman Roshi, during a heart-warming ceremony, installed me as the Abbess of Maitreya Abbey. At the end of the ceremony he gave me a *hossu*, a piece of wood with a white horse tail at the end. This whisk is an implement that Zen Masters use sometimes, especially during ceremonies. He asked me if I wanted to say something.

"Wow!" I said. "It has taken me my whole life to get one of these, while my mare always had hers and uses it freely to swat flies." Then, I swatted with my newly-given hossu as if I was removing my own flies from my back. I later heard that Bernie really liked my answer.

Great Mountain Zen Center at Maitreya Abbey hosts Zen retreats monthly, Great Heart Way programs and retreats and workshops on the Goddess Practices. Please come join us!

Part II

The Goddess Practices

14

The Loss of the Feminine

Tsultrim Allione writes in *Women Rising*:

> The loss of feminine qualities is an urgent psychological and ecological issue in modern society. It is a painful loss in our emotional lives and a disastrous loss for the safety of life on earth. In woman, it affects her central identity; and in man it affects his ability to feel and value. The loss of the feminine in man causes him to feel moody and lonely. In woman, it causes her to lose faith in herself. We are slowly awakening to the crisis of the earth and the effect of the loss of the sacred feminine, but few people understand that the causes of the crisis have spiritual values at their roots – values of the sacred as immanent, imbued in all life, and all life as interdependent.… It is by empowering the sacred feminine and by listening to the earth as she cries to communicate with us that we will ultimately heal.

In order to help reestablish the female deity to Her place in the sky and in our psyches, as our role model, and as our own enlightened image of unconditional love and compassion, I offer the Goddess Practices. I have adapted these practices from the book written by Tenzin Wangyal Rinpoche, *Healing with Form, Energy and Light: The Five Elements in Tibetan Shamanism, Tantra and Dzogchen*.

In one of the retreats I attended with Tenzin Wangyal Rinpoche, a contemporary teacher in the Bön *Vajrayana* tradition, he mentioned that he was allowed to put into the world practices that have been kept secret for many centuries and he hopes that they are used to create goodness in the world. Vajrayana is a school of Buddhism based on a set of texts that are referred to as Buddhist tantras. The Goddess Practices are at the very heart of my Zen practice. When I attended a retreat with Rinpoche, I had requested an individual meeting to tell him this in person, but his attendant told me that individual meetings were not available. Only group meetings were possible. We had about half an hour or so for eight or ten people to ask him a question. I had so much that I wanted to say that I didn't find this a propitious time to tell him how important the Goddess Practices were to me.

At the end of each retreat with him, there was always a talent show. During the talent show I presented a large tempera painting, about seven feet by five feet in size, of Space Goddesses carrying healing nectar in their vases and pouring this nectar into the crown chakras of people who were suffering. I had cut this painting in three lengthwise pieces and had taken each piece to a shop to be protected with clear film. Then I rolled all the pieces together to make them fit inside my luggage. I also brought wide transparent plastic tape with me to put the pieces back together at Serenity Ridge Retreat Center in Charlottesville, Virginia.

Once there, I asked a handyman who worked at the retreat center if he had some hooks and wire to hang the painting for my presentation. I had volunteered to be the person in charge of the decorations for the talent show. I was able to hang the painting behind the scenery and cover it with a big sheet until it was my turn in the talent show.

When my turn arrived, I presented myself, some of my experiences and my search for the Woman of Light throughout my life in a poetic way. I said that I had found what I was looking for in the Goddess Practices that Rinpoche had presented in his book. I showed the painting. Many people were delighted and Rinpoche himself seemed amused. At the end of my presentation, I expressed my gratitude to the Tibetan Bön tradition for having kept these practices safe for us today.

Many people came up to me after the presentation and told me how much they liked the painting, and asked me if I would consider donating the painting to the Retreat Center. I happily contemplated that idea, but they were going to be under construction soon. A woman told me that the painting was probably going to be forgotten in a cluttered closet and advised me to take it with me. I took it home and to this day it is still rolled up on a shelf in my office.

In the early morning, Rinpoche was performing the last ritual of the retreat for those of us who had to leave sooner. This was an opportunity for the participants to give some donation to the teachers and for the Rinpoche to bestow blessings. When it was my turn and after dropping my donations in the basket, I approached Rinpoche. At the retreat center, I had bought a red silk *khata*, a piece of fabric like a scarf often offered at Tibetan Buddhist ceremonies of greeting or parting, that I still keep in my room over my bed. Rinpoche blessed the khata for me and placed it tenderly around my neck. Then he adjusted my winter cap, told me to keep warm and wished me a good journey. I felt we had an understanding.

The Goddess Practices came to my life at the right time. Something clicked inside when I found them, as if the final piece of my life puzzle has been completed. I am certain I had done these practices in an ancient past and that it was the Goddess of the Space's Light who had manifested to me when I was little. She is a manifestation of my own true nature. I had yearned all of my life for the degree of healing that these practices can bring to the body and soul.

I believe the Goddess Practices were developed in the time of the Great Mother religion. John Jackson, who helped Tenzin Wangyal Rinpoche establish the Ligmincha Institute and who teaches these practices, confirms that we can only speculate about their origins. In an email he said, "The Tibetan texts from which the elements practices are drawn are from the seventh century CE, but they probably precede that by many centuries, and were passed down orally."

My own understanding is that during the time of the persecutions they passed to India in the form of Tantric Buddhism, and entering in Tibet they were guarded for posterity by the Bön tradition.

Now they come to light in this age when the Sacred Feminine needs to be nourished more than ever for the benefit of the Earth and all sentient beings.

I have been doing these practices for more than a decade, and after so many years they have gradually evolved inside me. In the versions I offer here, I have expanded the visualizations and adapted them to the Western mind.

It is important to remember that when the Sacred Feminine was suppressed, it was suppressed in people of all genders. Today people of all genders who want to feel more in harmony with their feminine side can perform these practices. People of all genders will be grounded in their innate value. When we invoke the goddesses or the enlightened ones, it is important to note that we are calling on energies that are already inside of us. By calling them we are awakening them. Inside and outside are not separate.

The Goddess Practices balance the elements of earth, water, fire, air and space inside our body, energy and heart-mind. You can feel the effect in your body soon after you have performed one complete round of the practices. Most people at the beginning have difficulty with the visualization. I recommend that you get a piece of fabric, paper or clothing of the color of the Goddess that you are invoking. Seeing the actual color will help you more effectively to visualize the color of each Goddess.

15

Overview of the Goddess Practices

It is important to have an overview of the Goddess Practices before you start practicing them. This overview will make it clear and simple. Each practice has five parts. During parts I, II, IV and V, we chant the different sounds according to each Goddess. It is the same repetitive pattern and is easy to follow. In part III, we visualize retrieving the healing light of the different elements.

We start each Goddess Practice by opening our hearts with a *metta*, or loving kindness, prayer for the welfare of all beings. We end each Goddess Practice with a dedication of merit to benefit all beings and to grant us a long life of service. You can recite both of these prayers.

I. Transformation of the Body
    A) Original Sound
    B) Sound of the Goddess
    C) Sound of the Elements

II. Transformation of Energy
    A) Original Sound
    B) Sound of the Goddess
    C) Sound of the Elements

III. Healing Vizualizations

IV. Transformation of the Mind
    A) Original Sound
    B) Sound of the Goddess
    C) Sound of the Elements

V. Transformation of the Soul
    A) Original Sound
    B) Sound of the Goddess
    C) Sound of the Elements

Qualities and Sounds of Each Element

In the next chart you can find a summary of the qualities, colors, symbols, defilements, corresponding organs and the different sounds for each element. In general, these sounds are not translated. They do not make up sentences or words. They are sacred sounds that hold essences within the sound. However, there is a symbolic meaning within each sound. For example, when we invoke the earth with MA KHAM, MA is calling the Mother, KHAM is the essence of earth itself in sound. So literally we are calling out to Mother Earth, asking for her blessings. MAM is the essence of water in sound, YAM the essence of air, and so on. They are written in Sanskrit. At the beginning of each Goddess Practice, I go into detail on how to pronounce these sounds.

EARTH: The organ is the spleen. The qualities are groundedness, strength and security. The benefits are overcoming pride and arrogance and experiencing the wisdom of equanimity. The symbol is a mountain and the color is radiant yellow-gold.

Original Sound: MA KHAM
Sound of the Goddess: KHAM LA ZI KYE LE DU

WATER: The organs are the kidneys. The qualities are calmness, comfort and openness. The benefits are overcoming anger and experiencing mirror-like wisdom. The symbol is a vast and calm lake. The color is deep blue.

Original Sound: A MAM
Sound of the Goddess: MAM DANG RA MAM TING DU

FIRE: The organ is the liver. The qualities are warmth, creativity and generosity. The benefits are overcoming attachment, desire and greed, and experiencing discerning wisdom. The symbol is a volcano. The color is bright red.

Original Sound: A RAM
Sound of the Goddess: RAM TSAG TANG NE RAM DU

AIR: The organs are the lungs. The qualities are flexibility, freshness and peacefulness. The benefits are overcoming envy and jealousy, and experiencing all-accomplishing wisdom. The symbol is the fresh wind. The color is bright green.

Original Sound: MA YAM
Sound of the Goddess: YAM YAM NI LI THUN DU

SPACE: The organ is the heart. The qualities are spaciousness, clarity and ease. The benefits are overcoming ignorance, experiencing unconditional love and the wisdom of emptiness. The symbol is the sky. The color is white or light blue.

Original Sound: MA A
Sound of the Goddess: A MU YE A KAR A NIA

The sound of all the elements is chanted after the other sounds and is always the same one; therefore, I only write it here once.

Sound of All the Elements: A YAM RAM MAM KHAM BRUM DU

How Do the Goddess Practices Work?

The Goddess Practices work by redirecting the energy of the thinking mind to create an inner space in which you can be at ease and open to receive the healing energies of your own awakened nature. During the practices, you will be guided on how to use the powers of concentration of your conceptual mind to connect with your own healing energies symbolized by the different goddesses.

Our feelings and emotions are always an expression of our own compassionate energy that is constantly arising from our deepest nature. When this energy gets obstructed or encumbered due to our reactivity, it gives rise to the unwholesome energies of pride and arrogance; anger and hatred; greed and attachment; jealousy and envy; ignorance and fear. Our usual tactic is to freeze the energy that naturally emanates from our deepest nature due to our habits of attraction and revulsion. We grasp at emotional energies that we judge as good feelings and we try to avoid or push away emotional energies that we consider to be uncomfortable or painful. Then the natural arising compassion solidifies and no longer flow in a beneficial way. The Goddess Practices are skillful means to begin to allow this conceptualized emotional energy to return to its natural flow. These practices are here to help us unfreeze the ways in which we have solidified our own emotional energy, and enable that energy to flow again in its natural form manifesting the five wisdoms.

The Goddess of the Earth's Light helps to transform pride and arrogance into the wisdom of equanimity. The Goddess of the Water's Light helps to transform anger and hatred into mirror-like wisdom, which is a wisdom that helps us see clearly without the projection of the ego mind. The Goddess of the Fire's Light helps to transform attachment and greed into the wisdom of discernment. The Goddess of the Air's Light helps to transform envy and jealousy into all-accomplishing wisdom, which is the wisdom to accomplish our deeper purpose on this Earth. The Goddess of the Space's Light helps to transform ignorance and fear and to realize the endless spring of unconditional love in our own hearts.

When and How to Do the Goddess Practices

Depending on how much interest you have, you can do each Goddess Practice daily, weekly or monthly. If this is your first time doing these practices and you have a lot of interest, you can do one elemental practice daily, every few days or weekly. Or you can do each Goddess Practice once a week or once a month. You can do them by themselves or accompanied by the preparatory practice, as described in the next chapter. Best of all, you can adjust the practices at your own pace. However, it is important to do these practices in the order given in order to start with the denser elements and then transition to the more ethereal ones: earth, water, fire, air and space. I recommend not doing more than one elemental Goddess Practice in a day. It is important to allow your body, energy and heart-mind to absorb the experience thoroughly.

I got started by doing one element each day for a week, then moving on to the next element. So, Earth every day for a week, then Water every day for a week, and continuing on through the sequence, always with only one element per day. It will take five weeks to move through the whole cycle of elements. Then you could move on to one a day...Earth one day, Water the next, and so on.

How to Visualize and Where to Do the Practices

When you chant, try to chant from your heart center. Call the Goddess with feeling. You are calling the Goddess to come to you and to arise in your inner space! You can call aloud or silently. It is better to be in a place where you won't be disturbed. These are visualization practices. At the beginning, in order to visualize you have to use your imagination. It will help if you color the Goddess of each element from the pages given for coloring at the end of this book and then place that colored page in front of you when you are doing the practices. For example, you can color the Earth Goddess bright yellow, the Water Goddess bright blue, the Fire Goddess bright red, the Air Goddess bright green, and the Space Goddess light blue. You can also wear a piece of clothing of the same color of the Goddess that you are invoking, as I mentioned before. The Goddesses are of luminous colors. You can have a glimpse of this transparent luminosity, as I mentioned before, by buying a piece of fabric, not too thick, of the color of the Goddess that you are invoking. Silk, rayon or thin cotton would work. Then hang it over a window so you can see its transparency. Each Goddess Practice is a guided meditation. After each instruction given, close your eyes and imagine what you just read. You do not need to see precisely. To see vaguely is good at the beginning. Visualization improves with practice.

Many times during the Goddess Practices it says, "Feel that your body is free from illnesses and obstructions," but you might not be able to feel this. Can you imagine yourself feeling this instead of your habitual perspective?

I would recommend that you do the Goddess Practices if you feel a connection to them. They might be for you or they might not be for you, and that is perfectly fine as well. The Goddesses of the elements are made of light and they represent the enlightened essence of the elements. We are used to thinking in opposites, in contraries. The mystic poet Rumi said: "Out beyond ideas of wrongdoing and rightdoing there is a field. I'll meet you there." Actually this is a very large field. It is so large that it is not limited by concepts of right and wrong, black and white, real and unreal. I cannot say that the Goddesses are real and neither can I say that they are unreal. They belong to that field of infinite possibilities. Once you have your own experience of the Goddesses and you have learned to visualize them, then you can tell me, are they real or unreal?

How to Chant

The sounds of the Goddesses are mantras. A *mantra* is a sacred utterance, a numinous sound, a syllable. The earliest mantras were composed in Vedic Sanskrit by Hindus in India and are at least 3000 years old.

Connect with your heart before you chant. It is important to use your heart energy to call the Goddess. Sit in a comfortable meditation posture and inhale and exhale a few times from your heart center in the middle of your chest at the level of your physical heart. Focus yourself here for three minutes. Then do the chanting and enjoy it. I recommend that you use your natural pitch and monotonic sounds. However, there is no wrong way to do it. If you feel yearning to unite with the Goddess, you can put this energy of yearning into your chant. If you feel love for the Goddess, you can put that love energy into your chanting. If you do not feel any of the above, that is okay too. Use any energy that is available to you.

Zen and Goddess Practice

As Buddhism migrated east from India, it adapted to the mind and culture of each country in which it took root. In India, it evolved from a focus on one's individual liberation to include the liberation of all beings. The new form was called Mahayana Buddhism or Great Vehicle Buddhism and it created the notion of the bodhisattva as the ideal of one who devotes oneself to awakening all beings before oneself.

When Indian Mahayana Buddhism migrated to China, it merged with Taoism and created Zen Buddhism which was further refined in Japan with its culture of the samurai and the esthetic arts of tea, flower arranging and calligraphy.

When Zen Buddhism arrived in the United States in the twentieth century, it took on at least three characteristics that distinguish it from the Buddhism of Japan, Korea and other countries of origin. These differences include: (1) a preponderance of lay people practicing in the US in contrast to the preponderance of monastics and priests in Asia; (2) women and men practice as equals in the United States whereas women are in an inferior position in Asia; and (3) Americans are vastly more concerned with their emotional and psychological well-being as part of practice. That element is often ignored in Japan.

These elements challenged the patriarchal heritage of Zen and gave rise to an interest in a lineage of women adepts. Veneration of the Goddess in Zen is a natural consequence of these changes. Women are awakening to their expression of the feminine wisdom of Zen and to the re-discovery of the Sacred Feminine in and as themselves.

The Importance of Goddess Practice for the Time of Death

The practice of the elemental Goddesses can be heartwarming at the time of death. During the process of death, the elements that form the body dissolve from grosser to subtler: earth, the hard substance of the body; water, fluids of the body; fire, heat; air, energy and movement. When we feel that the body becomes heavier and weaker, the dissolution of the earth element commences; we can let go of ourselves completely in the hands of the grounding love of the golden Earth Goddess. When the water element dissolves, we can let go of ourselves in the loving calmness of the blue Water Goddess. When the dissolution of the fire element starts, we can let ourselves go in the warming love of the red Fire Goddess. When we feel difficulty in breathing, we can let ourselves go in the peaceful love of the green Air Goddess. When our inner dissolution begins with the manifestation of the ground luminosity or clear light, we can let ourselves go completely in the unconditional love of the Space Goddess. This is a revelation of one's fundamental nature, which is also the fundamental nature of all phenomena. It is believed that one can be liberated right at this moment if one can recognize the clear light to be one's own nature and unite with it into a state of primordial purity. If one can recognize the clear light for what it really is, one will respond to it naturally like a child running into her mother's arms, the Goddess of Space, the Goddess of Unconditional Love. However, if one does not recognize the clear light, the mind enters the blackout state of the Bardo, the intermediate passage between death and rebirth.

Goddess Practice and Lucid Dreaming

Once you are very familiar with the Goddess Practices, they might help you to have a lucid dream. A lucid dream is when we are aware and conscious during a dream without waking up. If in a dream you see the color yellow, blue, red, green, pale blue or white, these colors will remind you about the Goddess Practice. If this happens, you could transform into one of the Goddesses and experience some sort of healing during the dream or perform healing actions for others.

16

Preparation for the Goddess Practices

Before you start the Goddess Practices, if you have the time, you can first prepare your heart-mind, energy and body to receive the Goddess' light. It is like preparing the soil before planting the seeds. This preparation takes about 15 minutes. You can do it by itself or before starting each of the Goddess Practices. Each Goddess Practice takes about half an hour. If you do this preparation before doing one of the Goddess Practices, it will take you about 45 minutes to do both.

Sit in meditation posture or comfortably in a chair or sofa, and perform the following visualizations and prayers. It is okay to take this lightly or more seriously, but in any case, enjoy it.

This preparatory practice, adapted from the Bön tradition, consists of four different invocations. During the first invocation, we will also be doing some heart purifications and empowerments.

1. The Enlightened Ones
   a. Heart Purification by: fire, wind and water
   b. Kanzeon Empowerments: body, energy and heart-mind
2. The guardians, planets and stars
3. Spirits of the area
4. All beings

Each invocation is followed by the Kanzeon chant from the Zen tradition. Kanzeon is another word for the Space Goddess, the Lady of Light, Virgin Mary, Avalokitesvara, Guan Yin, Kannon, or the bodhisattva of compassion. It is the sacred feminine, however you want to call Her. In this chant, She is called Kanzeon.

KANZEON! At one with Buddha,
All beings are one with Buddha
All beings awake to Buddha!
And to Buddha, Dharma, Sangha
Joyful, pure, eternal being!

Morning Heart is Kanzeon.
Evening Heart is Kanzeon.
This very moment arises from Heart.
This very moment is not separate from Heart.

As you repeat the following invocations, please visualize Kannon, the bodhisattva of compasion. You can use the drawings below. You can perform this practice aloud or silently. After each instruction or invocation, close your eyes and imagine what you just read. Your visualizations will improve with practice. Be patient and it will happen.

I want to humbly invoke all of the Enlightened Beings of the Universe to be with me today. I want to ask you for your blessings, guidance and support. I also want to ask you for my healing. As an offering to you, I will chant the Kanzeon.

Close your eyes and visualize the Enlightened Beings any way it comes to you or you can use the drawing to the left. Then chant or recite the Kanzeon.

Color the enlightened ones pale yellow. Larger image at back of book.

Now visualize Kanzeon, Goddess of Compassion. From the heart of the Goddess, flames of fire appear and reach your heart, purifying it. Visualize this fire entering your heart and burning away all of your defilements. Use your imagination. Whatever you can imagine is good enough. Every time you do this you will see some more.

You can color the heart and the flames translucent red.

Then visualize powerful wind energy emerging from Kanzeon's heart and blowing away the fire in your heart and any residues of defilements, obstacles or obscurations. Close your eyes and imagine this.

You can color the wind element translucent green.

Last, visualize a torrent of water pouring out from Kanzeon's heart, reaching your heart and washing away any remaining residues of defilements. Close your eyes and imagine this. Visualize your heart shining brightly.

You can color the water element translucent blue.

Now you are ready to receive Kanzeon's empowerments:

First, visualize that from Kanzeon's eyebrow center, that point between the eyebrows also known as third-eye chakra, a ray of pale yellow light emanates and as it reaches your eyebrow center, you receive an empowerment of body. Feel that your body and Her body become one and the same. Close your eyes and imagine this.

You can color the ray of light pale yellow.

Second, visualize a ray of red light from Kanzeon's throat chakra reaching your throat center; as it reaches your throat you receive an empowerment of energy. The throat chakra is located a little bit above the place where your neck meets your chest. Feel that your energy and her energy are one and the same. Close your eyes and imagine that.

You can color the ray of light pale red.

Third, visualize a ray of blue light from Kanzeon's heart center reaching your heart center. As it reaches it, you receive an empowerment of the heart-mind. Feel that your heart and her heart are one and the same. Close your eyes and imagine that. Feel unconditional love for all beings.

You can color the ray of light pale blue.

To finish this first part of the practice, visualize all of those fully enlightened beings who have gathered with you today as bright white or light-yellow light collected at the top of your head. Then this light will enter through your crown chakra, located on the top of your head, and descend through the central channel until it reaches your heart center. The central channel is one of the main subtle channels of the body. It is an energetic channel and cannot be measured or detected but it can be experienced directly by the practitioner. The central channel begins about four finger widths below the navel and rises straight through the center of the body to its opening at the crown of the head. The heart center is located in the center of your chest at the same level as your physical heart. Visualize your heart center being filled with this bright light. Close your eyes and imagine this. Chant or recite the Kanzeon prayer again and then continue reciting the invocations.

Second, I invoke all of the Guardians of the Sacred Teachings, the planets and the stars, and humbly ask you for your guidance and protection. As an offering to you, I will chant the Kanzeon. Chant or recite the Kanzeon prayer.

Third, I invoke the spirits of the area and humbly ask you not to harm me, to remove obstacles in my path and to pacify disturbances in my life. As an offering to you, I will chant the Kanzeon. Chant or recite the Kanzeon prayer.

Fourth, I invite all beings. For your happiness and protection, I offer this final chant of the Kanzeon. Chant or recite the Kanzeon prayer.

Color the enlightened ones light yellow. Color the other guests as you want.

17

Goddess of the Earth's Light

May all beings be happy,
May all be beings be safe,
May all beings be healthy,
May all beings be at ease.
And for the sake of all beings,
May we all be realized.

Her color is radiant yellow-gold. Her organ is the spleen. Her symbol is a powerful mountain. The qualities associated with Her are love, the feeling of being strong, secure and grounded on the Earth. The Earth Goddess can help you to overcome pride and arrogance and to manifest the wisdom of equanimity. Equanimity comes from absence of judgment. When there are no judgments, you can see everything with equanimity.

I. The Transformation of the Body

A) Original Sound:
MA KHAM

Chant this sound by elongating the syllables Maaaaaaaa Khaaaaaaaaam. Ma is pronounced as in Martin and Kha as in car.

As you chant the original sound of the Earth Goddess MA KHAM, imagine the luminous golden syllables appearing in the sky. Visualize or imagine how their golden light wraps around you. The MA KHAM syllables gathered above your head and enter your body through your crown chakra. See them descending into your central channel. Feel the sensations as the syllables of light enter your central channel reaching your sexual organs. See the yellow golden light radiating throughout your body, energy and heart. Your body is transformed into the golden body of the Earth Goddess. All the cells in your body are transformed into Her golden light. You feel loved, healthy, grounded, strong, secure, confident and golden.

Sing three times: MA KHAM

B) Sound of the Goddess:
KHAM LA ZHI KYE LE DU

Chant like Khamm Laaaaaa ziiiiii Kyeeeeee leeeeee duuuuuuuuuu.

La is pronounced as in L<u>a</u>rry; in Zhi the "i" is pronounced as an "e" like in <u>E</u>nglish; in Kye the "y" is pronounced as an "e" like in <u>E</u>nglish, and "e" as in <u>e</u>lephant; le as in l<u>e</u>t, du as in d<u>u</u>de.

As you visualize yourself as the golden body of the Earth Goddess, you sing her sounds. Feel that your body is free from all obstructions and illnesses.

Sing three times: KHAM LA ZHI KYE LE DU

C) Sound of All the Elements:
A YAM RAM MAM KHAM BRUM DU

In this mantra the "a" sounds like the "a" in c<u>a</u>r; the "u" in Brum and Du sounds like the "u" in d<u>u</u>de. As you chant you can elongate the syllables as you did before. There is no wrong way to do it.

As you continue visualizing yourself as the yellow body of the Earth Goddess, you sing the sounds of all the elements.

Sing three times: A YAM RAM MAM KHAM BRUM DU

II. The Transformation of Energy

A) Original Sound:
MA KHAM

As you sing the original sound MA KHAM, visualize the presence of another Earth Goddess in the spleen. The spleen is one of the largest organs of the lymphatic system. It is located on the top left side of the abdomen and sits below the diaphragm and near the stomach.

The Goddess in the spleen is of the same luminous golden light in which you have transformed, but smaller. You feel grounded, strong and secure. Feel that your body is free from obstructions and illnesses. Feel that you can manifest your highest potential.

Sing three times: MA KHAM

B) Sound of the Goddess:
KHAM LA ZHI KYE LE DU

As you sing the Sounds of the Goddess, you maintain the double visualization of yourself as the Earth Goddess and the smaller Earth Goddess in the spleen. Feel that your body is free from obstructions and illnesses. Feel that you can manifest your highest potential.

Sing three times: KHAM LA ZHI KYE LE DU

C) Sound of All the Elements:
A YAM RAM MAM KHAM BRUM DU

Continue to maintain both visualizations as you sing the sounds of all the elements. Continue to feel that your body is free from obstructions and illnesses. Feel that you can manifest your highest potential.

Sing three times: A YAM RAM MAM KHAM BRUM

III. Healing Visualizations

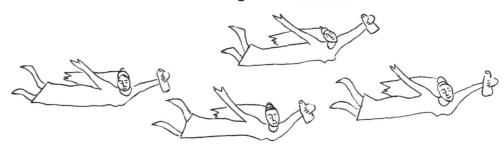

Be mindful of your breathing. With each exhalation, the Earth Goddess in the spleen sends out innumerable emanations of herself. See the Goddesses travelling through your body and leaving through the right nostril. As they leave, they carry from your body whatever energies you don't need or that are negative and they release those energies far away, dissolving them in pure space.

Visualize this cycle three times.

More Goddesses return to your body through your left nostril. Each carries a vase in her left hand with the bright golden light they have collected in the pristine and powerful mountains. They pour these golden lights in the spleen, healing it.

Visualize this cycle three times.

See more Goddesses leaving your body through your right nostril. Visualize them carrying from your body all toxic energy and dissolving those energies in faraway space.

Visualize this cycle three times.

Innumerable Goddesses go to the sacred lands and collect the pure yellow light in the vases they carry in their left hands. Once they have collected the golden light, they go and pour that light into places and incidents in the past where you lost elemental earth energy. We all have had traumatic or shocking incidents growing up. In those incidents we lost elemental energy. For example, it might come to you that you felt abused by someone and you felt disempowered. Anything that comes to your mind, work with that. If old trauma gets triggered, return to the awareness of yourself as the Earth Goddess. Your identity is now the Earth Goddess – loving, wise and powerful. The smaller Goddesses are emanations of yourself. The Goddesses pour the golden light upon those times and incidents from the past where there was hurt, shock or trauma. Feel the presence of the Goddesses – loving, wise and powerful. They heal the past and return to your inner child the qualities of groundedness, strength, confidence and security. Once you have visualized the Goddesses doing their healing, let all images go; do not hold onto them. Strengthen the visualization of yourself as the Earth Goddess as well as the visualization of the Earth Goddess in the spleen.

Visualize this cycle as long as needed.

More Goddesses leave your transformed Earth Goddess body, carrying from your body whatever is sick or toxic. They go to the lands of great potency and collect there the golden light of the earth element.

More Earth Goddesses return, entering the spleen and pouring what they have recovered into the spleen, healing it, and into the vase that the Goddess in the spleen carries in her left hand. Feel that your body is free from obstructions and illnesses. Feel that you can manifest your highest potential.

With each exhalation, Earth Goddesses travel outward through the right nostril; with each inhalation, Earth Goddesses return to you through the left nostril carrying the luminous golden light. The Goddesses pour these lights in the vase that the Earth Goddess in the spleen carries in her left hand.

Visualize this cycle three times.

With each exhalation, more Earth Goddesses leave to retrieve the pure luminous golden light. With each inhalation, golden Goddesses return, pouring the elemental yellow light they have retrieved into the spleen and into the vase that the Goddess in the spleen carries in her left hand.

Visualize this cycle three times.

Feel the spleen itself doing the breathing and healing in the process – exhaling from the spleen, inhaling into the spleen, breathing out the negativities, breathing in the golden light of the earth element.

See the golden light radiating throughout your body and your energy field.

Feel that your body is healed and that you can live up to your highest potential.

Visualize this cycle three times.

IV. The Transformation of The Mind

Exhale fully and then inhale deeply. See all Earth Goddesses returning with the inhalation. They enter the spleen, pouring out the elemental earth essence they have collected, and are absorbed back into the Goddess in the spleen. Feel the luminous golden light permeating your body and your energy field. Repeat this a few times.

A) Original Sound:
MA KHAM

As you sing the original syllables, MA KHAM, the Earth Goddess in the spleen becomes increasingly lively, vivid, and joyful. From the vase in her left hand, she pours the luminous golden light through your own crown chakra, and into your central channel, filling it up with golden light.

Feel the healing luminous golden light flowing in the central channel, from the crown chakra to the bottom of the central channel and reaching your sexual organs. Feel it flowing up and down your central channel, removing even the most subtle negativities and obstructions. Allow yourself to feel increasing peace and equanimity. The luminous golden nectar slowly accumulates in your heart center, filling it up.

Sing three times: MA KHAM

B) Sound of the Goddess:
KHAM LA ZHI KYE LE DU

As you chant the original syllables of the Goddess, feel the luminous golden light in your heart center. See the golden light radiating throughout your body and your energy field.

Sing three times: KHAM LA ZHI KYE LE DU

C) Sounds of All the Elements:
A YAM RAM MAM KHAM BRUM DU

As you sing the mantra of all the elements, visualize the healing golden light in the vase of the Goddess in your heart.

Sing three times: A YAM RAM MAM KHAM BRUM DU

V. Soul Healing

A) Original Sound:
MA KHAM

As we sing the original syllables of the Earth Goddess, MA KHAM, she rises up from your heart and pours the golden nectar into your own crown chakra. Experience the golden light flowing up and down your central channel and filling your heart center. This time the healing nectar becomes one with your soul. This is the deepest dimension of healing.

Sing three times: MA KHAM

B) Sound of the Goddess:
KHAM LA ZHI KYE LE DU

As you sing the sounds of the Goddess, feel all of your obstacles removed and all illnesses healed. Feel the luminous golden light radiating through your entire body and your energy field.

Sing three times: KHAM LA ZHI KYE LE DU

C) Sounds of All the Elements:
A YAM RAM MAM KHAM BRUM DU

Recite the sounds of all the elements and visualize the Earth Goddess dissolving in your heart. As she dissolves into your heart, feel the presence of equanimity radiating throughout your heart-mind. Bring forth equanimity in your daily life, your relationships with all of those around you, and the world.

Sing three times: A YAM RAM MAM KHAM BRUM DU

For the sake of our planet and all sentient beings,
May the earth element be balanced everywhere,
May equanimity pervade the ten directions,
And the three times.
May I serve all earthlings,
May I have a long and healthy life
To accomplish it.

Maha Prajna Paramita!

This concludes the practice of the Goddess of the Earth's Light.

18

Goddess of the Water's Light

May all beings be happy,
May all be beings be safe,
May all beings be healthy,
May all beings be at ease.
And for the sake of all beings,
May we all be realized.

Her color is deep blue. Her organs are the kidneys. Her symbol is a calm and vast lake. Her qualities are love, relaxation and openness. The Water Goddess can help you to overcome anger and manifest mirror-like wisdom. This is a wisdom that is not based on the ego mind, helping you see clearly without projection. Mirror-like wisdom is like a mirror that reflects everything. If you see someone that appears to be angry to the conditioned mind, mirror-like wisdom will reflect the underlying pain of that person. If you see someone being hateful, you see that person's underlying ignorance. When we usually see someone angry or hateful, we project our own aversion into that person. The mirror does not react to happiness or to anger. Mirror-like wisdom is the capacity to see clearly without reacting or projecting.

I. The Transformation of the Body

A) Original Sound:
A MAM

As you chant the original sound of the Water Goddess A MAM, see the deep blue syllables appear in the sky. Their blue light wraps around you. The A MAM syllables gather above your head and enter your body through your crown chakra. See them descending into your central channel. Feel the sensations as the syllables of deep blue light enter your central channel, reaching to your sexual organs and radiating the deep blue light throughout your body. Your body is transformed into the deep blue body of the Water Goddess. All the cells in your body are transformed into the luminous blue light of the Water Goddess. You feel loved, healthy, peaceful, relaxed and open.

Sing three times: A MAM

B) Sound of the Goddess:
MAM DANG RA MAM TING DU

Every "a" in this mantra sounds like the "a" in c<u>a</u>r. The "i" in Ting sounds like the "i" in t<u>i</u>n. The "u" in Du sounds like the "u" in d<u>u</u>de.

While you visualize yourself as the deep blue body of the Water Goddess, you sing her mantra. Feel that your body is free from all obstructions and illnesses.

Sing three times: MAM DANG RA MAM TING DU

C) Sound of All the Elements:
A YAM RAM MAM KHAM BRUM DU

As you continue visualizing yourself as the deep blue body of the Water Goddess, you sing the sounds of all the elements.

Sing three times: A YAM RAM MAM KHAM BRUM DU

II. The Transformation of Energy

A) Original Sound:
A MAM

As you sing the original sound, A MAM, visualize the presence of two other Water Goddesses in the kidneys – one in each kidney. The Goddesses in the kidneys are of the same deep blue light in which you have transformed, but smaller. You feel loved, healthy, peaceful, relaxed and open. Feel that your body is free from obstructions and illnesses. Feel that you can attain your highest potential.

Sing three times: A MAM

B) Sounds of the Goddess:
MAM DANG RA MAM TING DU

As you sing the sounds of the Water Goddess, maintain the triple visualization of yourself as the Water Goddess and two smaller Water Goddesses in the kidneys. Feel that your body is free from obstructions and illnesses. Feel that you can attain your highest potential.

Sing three times: MAM DANG RA MAM TING DU

C) Sounds of All the Elements:

A YAM RAM MAM KHAM BRUM DU

Continue to maintain the visualization of yourself as the Water Goddess with two small Goddesses in the kidneys, as you sing the mantra of all the elements. Continue to feel that your body is free from obstructions and illnesses and that you can attain your highest potential.

Sing three times: A YAM RAM MAM KHAM BRUM DU

III. Healing Visualizations

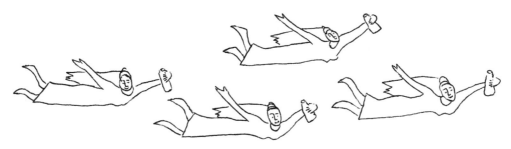

Be mindful of your breathing. With each exhalation, the Goddesses in the kidneys send out innumerable emanations of themselves.

See the Goddesses travelling through your body and leaving through your right nostril. As they leave, they carry from your body whatever energy you don't need or that is negative, and they release those energies in faraway space.

Visualize this cycle three times.

Deep blue Goddesses return to your body through your left nostril. In their left hands, they carry vases filled with the deep blue light they have collected in the pristine lakes and deep oceans. They pour this luminous blue light into the vases that the Goddesses in the kidneys hold in their left hands and into the kidneys, healing them.

Visualize this cycle three times.

See more deep blue Goddesses leaving your body through your right nostril. Visualize them carrying from your body all toxic energy and dissolving those energies in faraway space.

Visualize this cycle three times.

Innumerable deep blue Goddesses go to the deep oceans and collect the deep blue light in the vases they carry in their left hands. Once they have collected the luminous blue light, they go to places and incidents in the past where they know you lost elemental water energy. Feel the presence of the Goddess in yourself as loving, wise and powerful.

The Goddesses pour the deep blue light into those times and incidents from the past where there was trauma, hurt or shock. Most of us have had traumatic or shocking incidents growing up. In those incidents we lost elemental energy. For example, a time when you had a fight with someone and you felt disempowered might come to your mind. Anything that comes to your mind, work with that. If old trauma gets triggered, strengthen the awareness of yourself as the Water Goddess. Your identity is now that of the Water Goddess – loving, wise and powerful. The smaller Goddesses pour the blue light upon those times and incidents from the past where there was hurt, shock or trauma. They heal the past and return to your inner child the qualities of peace, relaxation and openness. After the healing has been done, let the images go. Do not hold onto them. Strengthen the visualization of yourself as the Water Goddess as well as the visualization of the Goddesses in the kidneys. Visualize this cycle as long as needed.

More blue Goddesses leave your transformed Water Goddess body. They carry from your body whatever is unhealthy or toxic. They go to the pristine lakes and deep oceans and collect there the deep blue light of the water element.

More Water Goddesses return, entering the kidneys and pouring what they have recovered into the kidneys, healing them, and into the vases that the Goddesses in the kidneys carry in their left hands. Feel that your body is free from obstructions and illnesses. Feel that you can attain your highest potential.

With each exhalation, Water Goddesses travel outward through the right nostril; with each inhalation, Water Goddesses return to you through the left nostril carrying the luminous deep blue light. The Goddesses pour these lights into the vases that the Water Goddesses in the kidneys carry in their left hands.

Visualize this cycle three times.

With each exhalation, more Water Goddesses leave to retrieve the pure luminous deep blue light. With each inhalation, deep blue Goddesses return, pouring the elemental deep blue light they have retrieved into the kidneys and into the vases that the Goddesses in the kidneys carry in their left hands.

Visualize this cycle three times.

Feel the kidneys themselves doing the breathing and healing in the process: exhaling from the kidneys, inhaling into the kidneys, breathing out the negativities, breathing in the deep blue light of the water element.

See the deep blue light radiating throughout your body and your energy field. Feel that your body is healed and that you can live up to your highest potential.

Visualize this cycle three times.

IV. The Transformation of the Mind

Visualize all Goddesses returning with the inhalation. They enter the kidneys, pouring out the blue light they have retrieved, and are absorbed back into the Goddesses in the kidneys. Feel the blue light pervading the body and every element of experience.

Repeat this cycle three times.

A) Original Sound:
A MAM

As we sing the syllables A MAM, the Goddesses in the kidneys become one at the center of both kidneys. Then from the vase in her left hand she pours the deep blue light through your own crown chakra, into the central channel extending down to your sexual organs. Feel the deep blue light flowing in the central channel and into the sexual organs. Feel this deep blue light flowing up and down the central channel, removing even the most subtle obscurations and blockages. Feel increasing calm, comfort in the body and mirror-like wisdom. The deep blue light accumulates in the heart center, and then is integrated into consciousness.

Sing three times: A MAM

B) Sound of the Water Goddess:
MAM DANG RA MAM TING DU

As you sing the mantra of the Water Goddess, feel the deep blue light in your heart center integrating with your awareness until your awareness and the deep blue light merge completely. Feel that whatever needed healing is healed. Whatever needed strengthening is strengthened. Anger and hatred are dispelled and mirror-like wisdom manifests.

Sing three times: MAM DANG RA MAM TING DU

C) Sounds of All the Elements:
A YAM RAM MAM KHAM BRUM DU

Feel that your body is free from obstructions and illnesses and that you can manifest your highest potential, as you sing the sounds of all the elements.
A YAM RAM MAM KHAM BRUM DU

V. Soul Healing

A) Original Sound:
A MAM

As you sing the seed syllables of the Water Goddess, A MAM, she rises up from your heart and pours the deep blue light into your crown chakra. Experience the deep blue light flowing up and down your central channel and your sexual organs. This time the deep blue light becomes one with your soul. This is the deepest dimension of healing.

Sing three times: A MAM

B) Sound of the Goddess:
MAM DANG RA MAM TING DU

As you sing the mantra of the Water Goddesses, feel all of your obstacles removed, all illnesses healed, your deepest doubts clarified. Feel the luminous blue light radiating through your entire body. Experience this deep blue light merging with your consciousness. Your consciousness and the blue light become one.

Sing three times: MAM DANG RA MAM TING DU

C) Sound of All the Elements:
A YAM RAM MAM KHAM BRUM DU

Sing the sounds of all the elements and visualize the Water Goddess dissolving in your heart. As she dissolves into your heart, feel the presence of mirror-like wisdom radiating throughout your heart-mind. Bring forth mirror-like wisdom in your daily life, your relationships with all of those around you, and the world.

Sing three times: A YAM RAM MAM KHAM BRUM DU

For the sake of our planet and all sentient beings,
May the water element be balanced everywhere,
May mirror-like wisdom pervade the ten directions,
And the three times.
May I serve all earthlings,
May I have a long and healthy life
To accomplish it.

Maha Prajna Paramita!

This concludes the practice of the Goddess of the Water's Light.

19

Goddess of the Fire's Light

May all beings be happy,
May all be beings be safe,
May all beings be healthy,
May all beings be at ease.
And for the sake of all beings,
May we all be realized.

Her color is luminous red. The organ is the liver. Her symbol is a volcano. The qualities associated with her are love, warmth, creativity and generosity. The practice of the Fire Goddess can help you to overcome attachment and greed and to develop discerning wisdom. Discerning wisdom is an intuitive way to know what action to take without having to think about it. It is the intuitive way of knowing.

I. The Transformation of the Body

A) Original Sound:
A RAM

As you chant the original sound of the Fire Goddess A RAM, see the luminous red syllables appearing in the sky. Their red light wraps around you. The A RAM syllables gather above your head, entering your body through your crown chakra. See them descending into your central channel. Feel the sensations as the syllables of red light enter your central channel reaching down to your sexual organs. See the red light radiating throughout your body, energy and heart-mind. Your body is transformed into the red body of the Fire Goddess. All the cells in your body are transformed into the red light of the Fire Goddess. Feel her love, warmth, creativity and generosity.

Sing three times: A RAM

B) Sound of the Goddess:
RAM TSAG TANG NE RAM DU

As you sing the sound of the Fire Goddess, feel her love, warmth, creativity and generosity. Feel that you are free from negativities and all illnesses, healed. Feel that you can manifest your highest potential.

Sing three times: RAM TSAG TANG NE RAM DU

C) Sound of the Elements:
A YAM RAM MAM KHAM BRUM DU

As you continue visualizing yourself as the luminous red body of the Fire Goddess, sing the sounds of all the elements.

Sing three times: A YAM RAM MAM KHAM BRUM DU

II. The Transformation of Energy

A) Original Sound:
A RAM

As you sing the original sound A RAM, visualize the presence of another Fire Goddess in your liver. The liver is located on the right side of your abdomen under your rib cage. The Goddess in the liver is of the same red light in which you have transformed, but smaller. Feel her love, warmth, creativity and generosity. Feel that your energy is free from obstructions and illnesses. Feel that you can manifest your highest potential.

Sing three times: A RAM

B) Sound of the Goddess:
RAM TSAG TANG NE RAM DU

As you sing her sounds, maintain the double visualization of yourself as the Fire Goddess and a smaller Fire Goddess in the liver. Feel that your body is free from obstructions and illnesses. Feel that you can manifest your highest potential.

Sing three times: RAM TSAG TANG NE RAM DU

C) Sounds of All the Elements:
A YAM RAM MAM KHAM BRUM

Continue to maintain both visualizations as you sing the mantra of all the elements. Feel that your energy is free from obstructions and illnesses. Feel that you can manifest your highest potential.

Sing three times: A YAM RAM MAM KHAM BRUM

III. Healing Visualizations

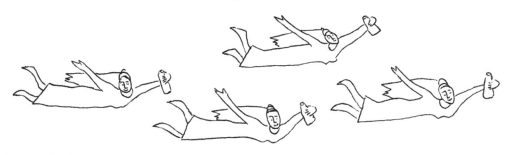

Be mindful of your breathing. With each exhalation, the Fire Goddess in the liver sends out innumerable emanations of herself.

See the Goddesses travelling through the channels of your body, leaving through the right nostril. As they leave, they carry from your body whatever energies you don't need or that are toxic. They release those energies far away, dissolving them in pure space.

Visualize this cycle three times.

More Goddesses are returning to your body through your left nostril. In the vase in each of their left hands, they carry the bright red light they have collected from the active volcanoes. They pour these red lights into the liver, healing it.

Visualize this cycle three times.

See more Goddesses leaving your body through your right nostril. Visualize them carrying from your body all toxic energies and dissolving those energies in faraway space.

Visualize this cycle three times.

Feel the presence of the Goddess as yourself – loving, wise and powerful. Visualize innumerable Goddesses leaving your transformed Fire Goddess body through your right nostril. The small Goddesses go to active volcanoes and collect the red light in the vases they carry in their left hands. Then they go to places and incidents in the past where you lost elemental red energy. The Goddesses pour the red light into those times and incidents from the past where there was trauma, hurt or shock. We all have had traumatic or shocking incidents growing up. In those incidents we lost elemental energy. For example, there might have been a time when someone accused you of something you didn't do, or some other event might come to your mind. Anything that comes to your mind, work with that. If old trauma gets triggered, strengthen the awareness of yourself as the Fire Goddess. Your identity is now that of the Fire Goddess – loving, wise and powerful. The smaller Goddesses pour the red light upon those

Roshi Ilia Shinko Perez

times and incidents from the past where there was hurt, shock or trauma. The red light is healing nectar. Visualize the Goddesses doing the healing. Let them act freely. They heal the past and return to your inner child the qualities of warmth, generosity and creativity. After the healing is done, let the images go. Do not hold on to them. Strengthen the visualization of yourself as the Fire Goddess, as well as the visualization of the Goddess in the liver.

Visualize this cycle three times or as long as needed.

More Goddesses leave your transformed Fire Goddess body carrying from your body whatever is negative or toxic. They go to the active volcanoes and collect there the red light of the fire element.

Fire Goddesses return, entering the liver and pouring what they have recovered into the liver, healing it, and into the vase that the Goddess in the liver carries in her left hand. Feel that your body is free from obstructions and illnesses. Feel that you can manifest your highest potential.

With each exhalation, Fire Goddesses travel outward through the right nostril carrying all toxic energy; with each inhalation Fire Goddesses return to you through the left nostril carrying the luminous red light. The Goddesses pour these lights into the vase that the Fire Goddess in the liver carries in her left hand.

Visualize this cycle three times.

With each exhalation, more Fire Goddesses leave your body carrying away all negative energy. With each inhalation, red Goddesses return, pouring the elemental red light they have retrieved into the liver and into the vase that the Goddess in the liver carries in her left hand.

Visualize this cycle three times.

Feel the liver itself doing the breathing and healing in the process – exhaling from the liver, inhaling into the liver, breathing out the negativities, breathing in the red light of the fire element.

See the red light radiating throughout your body and your energy field. Feel that your body is healed and that you can live up to your highest potential.

Visualize this cycle three times.

IV. The Transformation of the Mind

Exhale fully and then inhale deeply. See all Fire Goddesses returning with the inhalation. They enter the liver, pouring out the elemental fire essence they have collected, and are absorbed back into the Goddess in the liver. Feel the luminous red light permeating your body and your energy field. Repeat this a few times.

A) Original Sound:
A RAM

132

As we sing the original sound A RAM, the Fire Goddess in the liver becomes increasingly lively, vivid, and joyful. From the vase in her left hand, she pours the luminous red light through your own crown chakra, and into your central channel, filling it up with red light.

Feel the healing red light flowing up and down in your central channel, from the crown chakra to the bottom of the central channel, reaching your sexual organs as well. Feel the healing nectar removing even the most subtle negativities and obstructions. Allow yourself to feel increasing love, warmth and generosity. The luminous red nectar slowly accumulates in your heart center, filling it up.

Sing three times: A RAM

B) Sounds of the Fire Goddess:
RAM TSAG TANG NE RAM DU

As you sing the mantra of the Fire Goddess, feel the luminous red light in the heart center integrate with your awareness until your awareness and the red light merge completely.

Feel that whatever needs healing is healed. Whatever needed to be strengthened is strengthened. Greed and attachment are dispelled and discerning wisdom manifests.

Sing three times: RAM TSAG TANG NE RAM DU

C) Sound of All the Elements:
A YAM RAM MAM KHAM BRUM DU

As you continue visualizing yourself as the luminous red body of the Fire Goddess, you sing the sounds of all the elements combined.

Sing three times: A YAM RAM MAM KHAM BRUM DU

V. Soul Healing

A) Original Sound:
A RAM

As you sing the original sound of the Fire Goddess, A RAM, she rises up from your heart and pours the red nectar into your crown chakra. Experience the red light flowing up and down your central channel and filling your heart center. This time the healing nectar becomes one with your soul. This is the deepest dimension of healing.

Sing three times: A RAM

B) Sound of the Goddess:
RAM TSAG TANG NE RAM DU

As you sing the sounds of the Goddess, feel all of your obstacles removed and all illnesses healed. Feel the luminous red light radiating through your entire body and your energy field. Sing three times: RAM TSAG TANG NE RAM DU

C) Sounds of All the Elements:
A YAM RAM MAM KHAM BRUM DU

Chant the mantra of all the elements and visualize the Fire Goddess dissolving in your heart. As she dissolves into your heart, feel the presence of discerning wisdom radiating throughout your heart-mind. Bring forth discerning wisdom in your daily life, your relationships with all of those around you, and the world.

Sing three times: A YAM RAM MAM KHAM BRUM DU

> For the sake of our planet and all sentient beings,
> May the fire element be balanced everywhere,
> May discerning wisdom pervade the ten directions,
> And the three times.
> May I serve all earthlings,
> May I have a long and healthy life
> To accomplish it.

Maha Prajna Paramita!

This concludes the practice of the Goddess of the Fire's Light.

20

Goddess of the Air's Light

May all beings be happy,
May all be beings be safe,
May all beings be healthy,
May all beings be at ease.
And for the sake of all beings,
May we all be realized.

Her color is green. Her organs are the lungs. Her symbol is the fresh wind. The qualities associated with her are love, flexibility, freshness and peacefulness. The practice of the Air Goddess can help you to overcome jealousy and envy and to manifest all-accomplishing wisdom, which is the wisdom that can help you accomplish your true purpose in this life. All-accomplishing wisdom manifests when we are able to transform jealousy and envy. When we transform jealousy and envy, our conceptual mind opens up and a deeper wisdom manifests that allows us to accomplish our true purpose on this Earth.

I. The Transformation of the Body

A) Original Sound:
MA YAM

As you chant the original sound of the Air Goddess, see the luminous green syllables appearing in the sky. Their green light wraps around you. The green syllables gather above your head, entering your body through your crown chakra. See them descending into your central channel. Feel the sensations as the syllables of light enter your central channel, reaching down to your sexual organs. Then visualize the green light radiating throughout your body. Your body is transformed into the green body of the Air Goddess. All the cells in your body are transformed into the green light of the Air Goddess. You feel loved, fresh, flexible and peaceful.

Sing three times: MA YAM

B) Sound of the Goddess:
YAM YAM NI LI THUN DU

The "i" in "Ni" and "Li" is pronounced like the second "i" in India. The "th" in Thun is pronounced as a hard "t", as in tune. The "u" in Thun, as in dude.

Sing these sounds as you become the luminous Green Goddess. Visualize yourself luminous green. Experience the love, flexibility, freshness and peacefulness of the Air Goddess in your body. Visualize yourself radiating the green light.

Sing three times: YAM YAM NI LI THUN DU

C) Sounds of All the Elements:
A YAM RAM MAM KHAM BRUM DU

Sing the sounds of all the elements, as the Air Goddess. This will help you to seal the practice and to empower and stabilize the experience.

Sing three times: A YAM RAM MAM KHAM BRUM DU

II. The Transformation of Energy

A) Original Sound:
MA YAM

As you sing the original sound visualize the presence of two Air Goddesses in the lungs. The Goddesses in the lungs are of the same luminous green light into which you have transformed, but smaller. You feel loved, peaceful, flexible and fresh. Feel that your body is free from obstructions and illnesses. Feel that you can manifest your highest potential.

Sing three times: MA YAM

B) Sound of the Goddess:
YAM YAM NI LI THUN DU

As you sing the sounds of the Goddess, maintain the double visualization of yourself as the Air Goddess and two smaller Air Goddesses in the lungs. Feel that your body is free from obstructions and illnesses. Feel that you can manifest your highest potential.

Sing three times: YAM YAM NI LI THUN DU

C) Sounds of All the Elements:
A YAM RAM MAM KHAM BRUM DU

As you sing the sounds of all the elements, maintain the double visualization of yourself as the Air Goddess and two smaller Goddesses in the lungs.
Sing three times: A YAM RAM MAM KHAM BRUM DU

III. Healing Visualizations

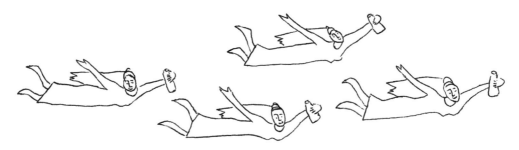

Be mindful of your breathing. With each exhalation, the Air Goddesses in the lungs send out innumerable emanations of themselves.

See the Goddesses travelling through the channels of your body and leaving through your right nostril. As they leave, they carry from your body whatever energies you don't need or that are toxic and they release those energies far away, dissolving them in pure space.

Visualize this cycle three times.

More Goddesses are returning to your body through your left nostril. They bring to you the bright green light they have collected from the high winds, in the vases they carry in their left hands. They pour this green light into the lungs, healing them.

Visualize this cycle three times.

See more Goddesses leaving your body through your right nostril. Visualize them carrying from your body all toxic energy and dissolving those energies in faraway space.

Visualize this cycle three times

Innumerable Goddesses go to the high winds and collect the pure green light in the vases they carry in their left hands. Once they have collected the green light, they pour it into places and incidents in the past where you lost elemental air energy. Feel the presence of the Goddesses, loving, wise and powerful, healing those events. We all have had traumatic or shocking incidents growing up when we felt disempowered. In those incidents we lost elemental energy. For example, a time when you felt abused by someone might come to your mind, or some other event. Anything that comes to your mind, work with that. If old trauma gets triggered, strengthen the awareness of yourself as the Air Goddesses. Your identity is now that of the loving, wise and powerful Air Goddesses. They pour the green light upon those times and incidents from the past where there was hurt, shock or trauma. If images appear in your mind let them be there, but after the healing is done let them go. Do not hold on to them.

Visualize this cycle three times.

More Goddesses leave your transformed Air Goddess body carrying from your body whatever is sick or toxic. They go to the winds above the highest mountains and collect there the green light of the air element.

More Air Goddesses return, entering the lungs and pouring what they have recovered into the lungs, healing them, and into the vase that each Goddess in the lungs carries in their left hand. Feel that your body is free from obstructions and illnesses. Feel that you can manifest your highest potential.

With each exhalation, Air Goddesses travel outward through the right nostril; with each inhalation, Air Goddesses return to you through the left nostril carrying the luminous green light. The Goddesses pour this light into the vases that the Air Goddesses in the lungs carry in their left hands.

Visualize this cycle three times.

With each exhalation, more Air Goddesses leave to retrieve the pure luminous green light. With each inhalation, green Goddesses return, pouring the elemental green light they have retrieved into the lungs and into the vases that the Goddesses in the lungs carry in their left hands.

Visualize this cycle three times.

Feel the lungs doing the breathing and healing in the process – exhaling from the lungs, inhaling into the lungs, breathing out the negativities, breathing in the green light of the air element.

See the green light radiating throughout your body and your energy field. Feel that your body is healed and that you can live up to your highest potential.

Visualize this cycle three times.

IV. The Transformation of the Mind

Exhale fully and then inhale deeply. See all Air Goddesses returning with the inhalation. They enter the lungs, pouring out the elemental air essence they have collected, and are absorbed back into the twin Goddesses in the lungs. Feel the luminous green light permeating your body and your energy field. Repeat this a few times.

A) Original Sound:
MA YAM

As we sing the original syllables MA YAM, the Air Goddesses in the lungs become increasingly lively, vivid, and joyful; becoming one at the center of your lungs, she rises up through your body. From the vase in her left hand, she pours the luminous green light through your own crown chakra, and into your central channel, filling it up with green light.

Feel the healing green light flowing in the central channel. See the green light radiating from the crown chakra to your sexual organs. Feel it flowing up and down your central channel, removing even the most subtle negativities and obstructions. Allow yourself to feel increasing love, peace, freshness and flexibility. The luminous green nectar slowly accumulates in your heart center, filling it up.

Sing three times: MA YAM

B) Sound of the Goddess:
YAM YAM NI LI THUN DU

As you chant the mantra of the Goddess, feel the luminous green light in your heart center. See the green light radiating throughout your body and your energy field.

Sing three times: YAM YAM NI LI THUN DU

C) Sounds of All the Elements:
A YAM RAM MAM KHAM BRUM DU

Continue to maintain both visualizations as you sing the mantra of all the elements. Continue to feel that your body is free from obstructions and illnesses. Feel that you can manifest your highest potential.

Sing three times: A YAM RAM MAM KHAM BRUM DU

V. Soul Healing

A) Original Sound:
MA YAM

As you sing the original sound of the Air Goddess, she rises up from your heart and pours the green nectar into your own crown chakra. Experience the green light flowing up and down your central channel and filling your heart center. This time the healing nectar becomes one with your soul. This is the deepest dimension of healing.

Sing three times: MA YAM

B) Sound of the Goddess:
YAM YAM NI LI THUN DU

As you sing the sounds of the Goddess, feel all of your obstacles removed and all illnesses healed. Feel the luminous green light radiating through your entire body and your energy field.

Sing three times: YAM YAM NI LI THUN DU

C) Sounds of All the Elements:
A YAM RAM MAM KHAM BRUM DU

Recite the mantra of all the elements and visualize the Air Goddess dissolving in your heart. As she dissolves into your heart, feel the presence of all-accomplishing wisdom radiating throughout your heart-mind. Bring forth all-accomplishing wisdom in your daily life, your relationships with all of those around you, and the world.

Sing three times: A YAM RAM MAN KHAM BRUM DU

For the sake of our planet and all sentient beings,
May the air element be balanced everywhere.
May all-accomplishing wisdom pervade the ten directions,
And the three times.
May I serve all earthlings,
May I have a long and healthy life
To accomplish it.

Maha Prajna Paramita!

This concludes the practice of the Goddess of Air's Light.

21

Goddess of the Space's Light

May all beings be happy,
May all be beings be safe,
May all beings be healthy,
May all beings be at ease.
And for the sake of all beings,
May we all be realized.

Her organ is the heart. Her color is white or pale blue light. Her image is the sky. Her qualities are spaciousness, clarity, ease and unconditional love. The practice of the Space Goddess will help you to transform ignorance into the wisdom of emptiness and unconditional love. Ignorance dwells in fear. This practice will help you to transform fear.

Space is the sacred element. It is pure potentiality. Everything arises from space and dissolves into space. When the space element is balanced in you, you have room in life; you can accommodate anything that arises. Doing these Goddess Practices regularly will help to balance and harmonize all of the elements within the space element in your body.

I. The Transformation of the Body

A) Original Sound:
MA A

As you recite the original sound of the Space Goddess MA A, from the infinite space the luminous white or light-blue syllables appear and their light washes over you and through you. The syllables gather above your head and descend through your crown chakra. Feel the sensations on your crown chakra as the syllables enter your body. Your body is instantaneously transformed into the light-blue body of the Space Goddess. All the cells in your body are transformed into soft blue light. You feel unconditional love, spaciousness, clarity and ease. The practice of the Space Goddess can help you to overcome ignorance and to develop the wisdom of emptiness and unconditional love for all beings

Sing three times: MA A

B) Sound of the Goddess:
A MU YE A KAR A NIA

As you visualize yourself as the light-blue body of the Space Goddess, you sing her sounds. Feel that your body is free from all obstructions and illnesses.

Sing three times: A MU YE A KAR A NIA

C) Sounds of the Elements:
A YAM RAM MAM KHAM BRUM DU

As you continue visualizing yourself as the light-blue body of the Space Goddess, you sing the sounds of all the elements.

A YAM RAM MAM KHAM BRUM DU

II. The Transformation of Energy

A) Original Sound:
MA A

As you sing her original sound MA A, visualize the presence of another Space Goddess in your heart, but smaller. The Goddess in your heart is of the same light-blue color in which you have transformed. Feel the spaciousness, clarity, ease, and unconditional love of the Space Goddess in your heart. Feel that your body is free from obstructions and illnesses. Feel that you can manifest your highest potential.

Sing three times: MA A

B) Sounds of the Goddess:
A MU YE A KAR A NIA

As you sing the mantra of the Goddess, you maintain the double visualization of yourself as the Space Goddess and the smaller Space Goddess in your heart. Feel that your body is free from obstructions and illnesses. Feel that you can manifest your highest potential.

Sing three times: A MU YE A KAR A NIA

C) Sounds of All the Elements
A YAM RAM MAM KHAM BRUM DU

Continue to maintain both visualizations as you sing the mantra of all the elements. Continue to feel that your body is free from obstructions and illnesses and that you can attain your highest potential.

Sing three times: A YAM RAM MAM KHAM BRUM

III. Healing Visualizations

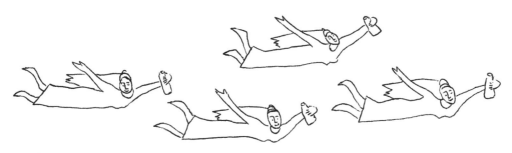

Visualize the Space Goddess in your heart transforming into a luminous white letter A radiating the five elemental lights of earth, water, fire, air and space. From this A, Goddesses from all the elements emanate. Leaving your body through your right nostril they travel into space. They return entering your body through your left nostril, and empty the elemental essences into the A in your heart.

Be mindful of your breathing. With each exhalation, the Space Goddess in the heart sends out innumerable Goddesses of all the elements – yellow, blue, red, green and white.

See the yellow, blue, red, green and white Goddesses travelling through the channels of your body and leaving through the right nostril. As they leave, they carry from your body whatever energies you don't need or that are toxic and they dissolve those energies in space.

Visualize this cycle three times.

More yellow, blue, red, green and white Goddesses are returning to your body through your left nostril. They carry the bright yellow, blue, red, green and white lights they have collected in the vases in their left hands. They pour these yellow, blue, red, green and white lights into the A in your heart. From the heart, the lights expand throughout your body, healing it.

Visualize this cycle three times.

See more yellow, blue, red, green and white Goddesses leaving your body through your right nostril. Visualize them carrying from your body all toxic and negative energies and dissolving those energies in space.

Visualize this cycle three times.

Innumerable yellow, blue, red, green and white Goddesses go to places and incidents in the past where you lost elemental space energy. Feel the presence of the Goddesses as yourself: loving, wise and powerful.

The yellow, blue, red, green and white Goddesses pour the yellow, blue, red, green and white lights on those times and incidents from the past where there was trauma, hurt or shock. They heal the past, returning to your inner child the qualities of unconditional love, spaciousness, clarity and ease. We all have had traumatic or shocking incidents growing up. In those incidents we lost elemental energy. For example, the times when you felt unloved, betrayed or abandoned might come to your mind. Anything that comes to your mind, work with that. If old trauma gets triggered, strengthen the awareness of yourself as the Space Goddess. Your identity is now that of the Space Goddess – loving, wise and powerful. The smaller yellow, blue, red, green and white Goddesses pour their lights upon those times and incidents from the past where there was hurt, shock or trauma. The multicolor elemental lights are the supreme healing nectar. Visualize the Goddesses doing the healing. Let them act freely. They heal the past and return to your inner child the gift of unconditional love. After the healing is done, let the images go. Do not hold on to them. Strengthen the visualization of yourself as the Space Goddess as well as the visualization of the A in the heart.

Visualize this cycle as long as needed.

More Goddesses leave your transformed Space Goddess body, carrying from your body whatever is negative or toxic. They go to all the pure elemental forces and collect the yellow, blue, red, green and white lights for you.

More yellow, blue, red, green and white Goddesses return, entering the A in the heart and pouring what they have recovered into the A in your heart, healing it. Feel that your body is free from obstructions and illnesses. Feel that you can manifest your highest potential.

With each exhalation, yellow, blue, red, green and white Goddesses travel outward through the right nostril; with each inhalation, yellow, blue, red, green and white Goddesses return to you through the left nostril carrying the luminous yellow, blue, red, green and white lights. The Goddesses pour these lights into the A in your heart.

Visualize this cycle three times.

With each exhalation, more yellow, blue, red, green and white Goddesses leave through your right nostril to retrieve the pure luminous yellow, blue, red, green and white lights. With each inhalation, yellow, blue, red, green and white Goddesses return, entering your body through the left nostril. They pour the yellow, blue, red, green and white lights into the A in your heart.

Visualize this cycle three times.

Feel your heart itself doing the breathing and healing in the process – exhaling from the heart, inhaling into the heart, breathing out the negativities, breathing in the yellow, blue, red, green and white lights of all the elements.

See the yellow, blue, red, green and white lights radiating throughout your body and your energy field. Feel that your body is healed and that you can live up to your highest potential.

Visualize this cycle three times.

IV. The Transformation of the Mind

Visualize all yellow, blue, red, green and white Goddesses returning with the inhalation. Yellow, blue, red, green and white Goddesses enter your heart, pouring the pure healing lights they have retrieved into the A in your heart. Then they are absorbed back into the A in your heart. Feel the pure yellow, blue, red, green and white lights pervading your body and your energy field.

A) Original Sound:

MA A

As you sing the original sound MA A, visualize how the Letter A transforms again into the Space Goddess. From the vase in her left hand, she pours the yellow, blue, red, green, and white lights into your crown chakra, filling your central channel. Feel these lights flowing in your central channel. See these lights radiating through your entire body – your organs, your breasts, your sexual organs, your intestines, your legs, arms, neck and head. See these lights healing your entire body. Feel increasing peace, bliss and well-being.

Feel the yellow, blue, red, green and white lights in your heart center radiating throughout your body and your energy field. Feel that whatever needed healing is healed and that you can live up to your highest potential. Unconditional love for the Earth and all beings becomes expansive as the sky.

B) Sound of the Goddess:

A MU YE A KAR A NIA

Abide in the state of unconditional love for the Earth and all beings as you sing the sounds of the Goddess.

Sing three times: A MU YE A KAR A NIA

C) Sounds of the Elements:

A YAM RAM MAM KHAM BRUM DU

As you continue visualizing yourself as the light-blue body of the Space Goddess, you sing the sounds of all the elements.

A YAM RAM MAM KHAM BRUM DU

V. Soul Healing

A) Original Sound:
MA A

As you sing the syllable mantra of the Space Goddess MA A, she rises up again from your heart and pours the yellow, blue, red, green and white nectar into your crown chakra.
Sing three times: MA A

B) Sound of the Goddess:
A MU YE A KAR A NIA

As you sing the sounds of the Goddess, experience the yellow, blue, red, green and white lights flowing down your central channel and filling up your heart center. The lights now become one with your soul, which is the deepest dimension of healing. The state of unconditional love for all beings emanates unhindered from your soul.
Sing three times: A MU YE A KAR A NIA

C) Sound of All the Elements:
A YAM RAM MAM KHAM BRUM DU

Feel that whatever needed healing is healed and that you can live up to your highest potential. Visualize the Space Goddess dissolving in your heart. Feel unconditional love for all beings becoming all-abiding. As she dissolves into emptiness, feel unconditional love radiating throughout your heart-mind and body. Manifest unconditional love in your daily life, in your relationships with all of those around you, and the world.

Sing three times: A YAM RAM MAM KHAM BRUM DU

For the sake of our planet and all sentient beings,
May the space element be balanced everywhere,
May unconditional love pervade the ten directions,
And the three times.
May I serve all earthlings,
May I have a long and healthy life
To accomplish it.

Maha Prajna Paramita!

This concludes the practice of the Goddess of the Space's Light.

Conclusion

When we look at the Earth from space we do not see the divisive lines of the different countries. After his flight on the Apollo 9, astronaut Rusty Schweickart wrote, "When you go around the Earth in an hour and a half, you begin to recognize that your identity is with that whole thing. That makes a change. You look down and you cannot imagine how many borders and boundaries you cross…. Hundreds of people killing each other over some imaginary line that you are not even aware of, you cannot even see it. From where you are, the planet is a whole and it is so beautiful and you wish you could take each individual by the hand and say: 'Look at it from this perspective. Look at what is important!'"

Our planet is at one edge of the Milky Way, a galaxy that travels among thousands of millions of galaxies. The Earth travels around the solar system at about sixty-seven thousand miles per hour, together with eight planets and countless moons, all gravitating around the sun in elliptic orbits. When our protective ego shell becomes lighter, we realize that we are the Earth and the entire universe is our home. Ancient people lived in harmony with the planet and the cosmos. Due to the air and light pollution it is impossible to see stars in many cities. When we lose connection with the cosmos we forget our place in the universe and lose our way.

One of the many illnesses that our planet is suffering from is the disconnection and alienation of people from each other and the sky. With many of us living separate lives in the comfort of our own homes, we can easily become numbed through our many electronic gadgets and become deaf to the cry of the many who are suffering. Many of us behave like blindfolded people playing a make-believe game that keeps us amused, while governments, oligarchs and corporations continue to destroy what is left of the planet and the voiceless beings. The very survival of the human race is being threatened. Oh! This beautiful and wondrous planet rotating together with eight other planets around the sun at the edge of the Milky Way! What have we done to it?

In a recent retreat in Madrid with the Great Heart Sangha, I made contact with the immortality of the clan. Ancestral teachings manifested as I entered deeply into the kirtan dance and my percussion on the classroom door. The music playing was of Krishna Das. Connecting with the ancestral energy through the dance was a revelation to me: I felt the ring of the ancestors surfacing from deep in the Earth. Then, at that moment, I realized that the ancient wisdom of the Native American people and all the people who had danced under the starry sky before us is still here. The wisdom of the clan never dies. When our ancestors passed away, they died into the clan's energy, and as they did, the clan continued to carry their wisdom-energy forward in rings of immortal space-time. This energy is still available to guide us in this turbulent time and to help us come back to a more grounded spirituality based on the love and nourishing of the Earth, the cosmos and all sentient beings.

> Once a monk on a pilgrimage met an old woman living alone in a hut. The monk asked, "Do you have any relatives?"
> She said, "Yes."
> The monk asked, "Where are they?"
> She answered, "The mountains, rivers, and the whole Earth, the plants and trees are all my relatives."
> [Caplow and Moon, *The Hidden Lamp*, Case 48]

All cycles of life and of nature are endless *dana*, or generosity. The sun warms the water which evaporates, the wind blows the water over the land, the wind and animals disperse the seeds of the plants, the mountains lift the air which drops its water on the seeds. Animals eat the seeds and in turn provide food to other animals, which when they die and decay add nutrients to the soil. Each season has something to give and something to receive. The Earth gives us everything we need to sustain and enhance our lives. What do we give in return?

> Chen was a laywoman who travelled far and wide, visiting famous masters. After she realized enlightenment, she composed the following verse:
>
> Up on the high slopes, I see only old woodcutters.
> Everyone has the spirit of the knife and the axe.
> How can they see the mountain flowers
> Reflected in the water – glorious red?
> [Caplow and Moon, *The Hidden Lamp*, Case 13]

The Lady of Light has been sealed in my heart since time immemorial. She has been my secret refuge, my guidance, my present and my future, and She would have remained secret if it had not been for what is happening to the Earth at this moment when we are at the brink of a climate catastrophe. She represented that which is most vulnerable in me, that which I didn't want to share with anyone for many decades because it is most intimate. But how could I let this precious planet with its wondrous creatures be destroyed without doing anything about it? Our lives and our very existence are a miracle: what do we want to do with it? When Hildegard of Bingen experienced union with the divine, she expressed it this way:

> I am the breeze that nurtures all things green…. I am the rain coming from the dew that causes the grasses to laugh with the joy of life.
> [Fox, *Hildegard of Bingen: A Saint for Our Times*]

Our climate mess originated with the creation of a technological civilization rooted in a denial of the Sacred Feminine and in the belief that nature (and women and minorities) existed only to be exploited. The Goddess practices that I present in the second part of the book aim to awaken the Sacred Feminine in people of all genders, therefore reawakening and strengthening the love for the Earth, the cosmos and all sentient beings. To quote the Dalai Lama's words, "The world will be saved by Western women." People of all genders: we can save the Earth together!

> The recognition of our essential non-separateness from the world, beyond the shaky walls erected by our fear and greed, is a gift occurring in countless lives in every generation. Yet there are historical moments when this recognition breaks through on a more collective level. This is happening now in ways that converge to bring into question the very foundation and direction of our civilization. A global revolution is occurring that is of such magnitude that people unacquainted with Buddhism are using a similar term. Many are calling it the Great Turning."
> [Macy, *World as Lover, World as Self*]

Now we are witnessing the dark night of our beloved planet. As I revise this book, the coronavirus is taking many lives. The suffering of the many beings is unfathomable. Feeling the deep grief for our deeply wounded planet is an intense pain that cuts through what is unnecessary in our lives. It is through the pain caused by the threat of losing our loved ones that we can wake up. Owning this pain, and experiencing it with presence, we can open up to the immensity of our heart. There is a Zen saying, "The universe is too small to contain our heart, but our heart contains the whole universe."

I have adapted the following verse from Brigit Anna McNeill:

> The tall rooted ones, the small green ones, the scaled, the furred, the winged and the slimy are wondering and waiting…. Will the two-leggeds return, weaving themselves back into the fabric of their nature or will they continue to plod, no longer seeing their home, no longer inhabiting their hearts?

It is important at times like this to cultivate the heart of gratitude for the great opportunity of being alive. The intrinsic purpose of life, like the writer Mathew Fox said, "It is not about living a happy life, it is about living a life that matters." A life that matters is what will ultimately make us happy. These are sacred times for each of us to re-evaluate our life and reconsider what we want to do with the rest of it.

May the Great Turning carry us,
From this time of great suffering and danger,
Into a time of renewal of the Earth's resources,
The equality of all human beings,
The rights for the voiceless creatures,
And the natural world.

May all beings be happy,
May all beings be safe,
May all beings be healthy,
May all beings be at ease.
And for the sake of all beings,
May we all be realized.

Maha Prajna Paramita!

Acknowledgments

Many beings have helped me in the writing of this book. I want to especially acknowledge my husband and unpaid agent, Gerry Shishin Wick. Shishin was with me on every step of this journey. His encouragement made writing this book a joyful process and his criticisms made it a better product. I could not have done it without him. Bows to Roshi Wendy Egyoku Nakao for her continuous support in bringing the Sacred Feminine into Zen practice. Thanks to my family, my mother, my siblings and my two sons, for providing support and encouragement. Tania Casselle served as the book's midwife. Her tireless effort guided me through the whole process of improving this book, editing it, helping me with the chapter structure and writing the synopsis, just to list a few of things she did. Sean Tetsudo Murphy helped me with his editing expertise and with guiding me through the first stages of the book. I am most grateful to Tania, Tetsudo and Michael Mui Lewis who did extensive and careful proofreading of the manuscript. My sister Izaskun Casado graciously shared her insight, inspiration and designer's eye. Thanks to Barry Wick, Charlie Jodo Meerts, Christine Fuan Jones, Kelly Seien Lusk, John Fugetsu Rueppel, Tony Hoetsu Falcone and Glenda Alicia Leung for feedback and proofreading. I also want to thank those who wrote endorsements for this book: Lama Tsultrim Allione, Wendy Egyoku Nakao, Eve Marko, Grace Schireson, Mirabai Starr; Judith Simmer-Brown, Joan Halifax, Andrew Harvey, Richard McDaniel and David Loy. Gassho to my students who participated in Goddess workshops and retreats and helped me refine the practices. A special shout-out to the women who ordained with me on this path: Kelly Seien Lusk, Heather Kuden Reid and Laura Ryuko Minks. And many thanks to my publisher John Negru, for his support, encouragement and his excellent work on the book design. It was a pleasure to work with him!

Bibliography

Aitken, Robert, 1993, *Encouraging Words*. New York: Pantheon.

Allione, Tsultrim. 2000. *Women of Wisdom*. Ithaca, NY: Snow Lion Publications.

_____. 2018. *Wisdom Rising: Journey into the Mandala of the Empowered Feminine*. Atria/Enliven Books.

Baring, Anne and Jules Cashford. 1993. *The Myth of the Goddess: Evolution of an Image*. London: Penguin.

Barnwell, Willis and Marvin Meyer (editors). 2003. *The Gnostic Bible*. Boston: Shambhala Publications.

Caplow, Florence and Susan Moon (editors). 2013. *The Hidden Lamp: Stories from Twenty-Five Centuries of Awakened Women*. Boston: Wisdom Publications.

Cleary, Thomas, trans. 2000. *Secrets of the Blue Cliff Record*. Boston: Shambhala Publications.

_____, trans. 1993. *The Flower Ornament Scripture: A Translation of the Avatamsaka Sutra*. Boston: Shambhala Publications.

Cornelius, Izak. 2004. *The Many Faces of the Goddess: The Iconography of the Syro-Palestinian Goddesses Anat, Astarte, Qedeshet, and Asherah c. 1500-1000 BCE* (Orbis Biblicus et Orientalis). Vandenhoeck & Ruprecht.

Davidson, Richard. 2006. *Did King David Rape Bathsheba? A Case Study in Narrative Theology.* Journal of the Adventist Theological Society: Vol. 17: Iss. 2, Article 4.

Dowman, Keith. 1996. *Sky Dancer: The Secret Life and Songs of the Lady Yeshe Tsogyel*. Ithaca, NY: Snow Lion Publications.

Fox, Matthew. 2012. *Hildegard of Bingen: A Saint for our Times*. Vancouver: Namaste Publishing.

Fox, Matthew, Skylar Wilson and Jennifer Berit Listug (editors). 2018. *Order of the Sacred Earth: An Intergenerational Vision of Love and Action*. Rhinebeck, NY: Monkfish Book Publishing Company.

Galland, China. 2007. *Longing for Darkness: Tara and the Black Madonna*. London: Penguin Books.

Gimbutas, Marija. 1989. *The Language of the Goddess*. New York: Thames and Hudson.

_____. 1999. *The Living Goddess*. (edited and supplemented by Miriam Robbins Dexter). Berkeley and Los Angeles, CA: University of California Press.

Hakuin Ekaku and Norman Wadell, trans. 2001. *Wild Ivy: The Spiritual Autobiography of Zen Master Hakuin*. Boston: Shambhala Publications.

Harvey, Andres and Carolyn Baker. 2017. *Savage Grace: Living Resiliently in the Dark Night of the Globe*. Bloomington, IN: iUniverse.

Jung, C.G. 1957. *The Collected Works of C.G. Jung Vol 11, Psychology and Religion: East and West*. Princeton, NJ: Princeton University Press.

Kapleau, Philip. 1980. *The Three Pillars of Zen*. Boston: Beacon Press.

Loy, David. 2018. *Ecodharma: Buddhist Teachings for the Ecological Crisis*. Boston: Wisdom Publications.

Macy, Joanna. 2007. *World as Lover World as Self*. Berkeley, CA: Parallax Press.

Maezumi, Hakuyu Taizan. 1978. *The Way of Everyday Life*. Los Angeles: Center Publications.

Mayo, Reverend Laura. 2019. By identifying abuse in Bible we can call out injustice in life. *Houston Chronicle*, February 15, 2019. https://www.houstonchronicle.com/life/houston-belief/article/By-identifying-abuse-in-Bible-we-can-call-out-13619414.php.

Mitchell, Stephen, trans. 1999. *Tao Te Ching: Lao Tzu: An Illustrated Journey*. New York: HarperCollins Publishers.

Pagels, Elaine. 2018. *Why Religion?: A personal Story*. New York: HarperCollins Publishers.

Perez, Ilia Shinko and Gerry Shishin Wick. 2006. *The Great Heart Way: How to Heal Your Life and Find Self-fulfillment*. Somerville, MA: Wisdom Publications.

Powell, William, translator. 1986. *The Record of Tung-Shan*. Honolulu: University of Hawaii Press.

Price, A.F. and Wong Mou-Lam. 1990. *The Diamond Sutra and the Sutra of Hui Neng*. Boston: Shambhala Publications.

Schireson, Grace. 2009. *Zen Women: Beyond Tea Ladies, Iron Maidens and Macho Masters*. Boston: Wisdom Publications.

Shibiyama, Zenkei. 1974. *Zen Comments on the Mumonkan*. New York: Harper & Row.

Stevens, John. 1993. *Three Zen Masters: Ikkyu, Hakuin, Ryokan*. New York: Kodansha America, Inc.

Stone, Merlin. 1976. *When God was a Woman*. New York: Harcourt, Brace Jovanovich Publishers.

Stuckey, Johanna 2007. The Holy One, Qedesh[et], lady of heaven, mistress of all the gods, eye of Ra, without her equal. *The MatriFocus, Cross-Quarterly for the Goddess Woman*, Lammas 2007, Vol 6-4, http://www.matrifocus.com/LAM07/spotlight.htm

Taylor, Therese. 2008. *Bernadette of Lourdes: Her life, death and visions*. London: Burns & Oates.

Tisdale, Sallie. 2006. *Women of the Way: Discovering 2000 Years of Buddhist Wisdom*. San Francisco: Harper Collins Publishers.

Waddell, Norman, translator. 1999. *Wild Ivy: The Spiritual Autobiography of Zen Master Hakuin*. Boston: Shambhala Publications.

Wangyal, Tenzin Rinpoche. 2002. *Healing with Form, Energy and Light: The Five Elements in Tibetan Shamanism, Tantra, and Dzogchen*. Ithaca, NY: Snow Lion Publications.

Watts, Alan. 1977. *Tao: The Watercourse Way*. New York: Pantheon.

Wick, Gerry Shishin. 2005. *The Book of Equanimity: Illuminating Classic Zen Koans*. Boston: Wisdom Publications.

———. 2015. *My American Zen Life*. Eugene, OR: Scrivana Press.

The Images

The Enlightened Beings
Color the enlightened ones pale yellow.

The Four Guests
Color the enlightened ones light yellow. Color the other guests as you want.

Goddess of the Earth's Light
Her color is radiant yellow

Goddess of the Water's Light
Her color is deep blue

Goddess of the Fire's Light
Her color is luminous red

Goddess of the Air's Light
Her color is green

Goddess of the Space's Light
Her color is white or pale blue

CPSIA information can be obtained
at www.ICGtesting.com
Printed in the USA
BVHW092304100822
644334BV00006B/74